D1074877

ADOLESCENT ANGER CONTROL

Pergamon Titles of Related Interest

Apter/Goldstein YOUTH VIOLENCE: Programs and Prospects
Kirby/Grimley UNDERSTANDING AND TREATING
ATTENTION DEFICIT DISORDER
Plas SYSTEMS PSYCHOLOGY IN THE SCHOOLS
Santostefano COGNITIVE CONTROL THERAPY WITH
CHILDREN AND ADOLESCENTS
Wielkiewicz BEHAVIOR MANAGEMENT IN THE SCHOOLS:
Principles and Procedures

Related Journals
(Free sample copies available upon request)

CHILDREN AND YOUTH SERVICES REVIEW
CLINICAL PSYCHOLOGY REVIEW
JOURNAL OF CHILD PSYCHOLOGY AND PSYCHIATRY

PSYCHOLOGY PRACTITIONER GUIDEBOOKS

EDITORS

Arnold P. Goldstein, Syracuse University
Leonard Krasner, SUNY at Stony Brook
Sol L. Garfield, Washington University

ADOLESCENT ANGER CONTROL

Cognitive - Behavioral Techniques

EVA L. FEINDLER
Adelphi University

RANDOLPH B. ECTON
Sagamore Children's Psychiatric Center

PERGAMON PRESS
New York Oxford Beijing Frankfurt
São Paulo Sydney Tokyo Toronto

Pergamon Press Offices:

U.S.A.	Pergamon Press, Maxwell House, Fairview Park, Elmsford, New York 10523, U.S.A.
U.K.	Pergamon Press, Headington Hill Hall, Oxford OX3 0BW, England
PEOPLE'S REPUBLIC OF CHINA	Pergamon Press, Qianmen Hotel, Beijing, People's Republic of China
FEDERAL REPUBLIC OF GERMANY	Pergamon Press, Hammerweg 6, D-6242 Kronberg, Federal Republic of Germany
BRAZIL	Pergamon Editora, Rua Eça de Queiros, 346, CEP 04011, São Paulo, Brazil
AUSTRALIA	Pergamon Press (Aust.) Pty., P.O. Box 544, Potts Point, NSW 2011, Australia
JAPAN	Pergamon Press, 8th Floor, Matsuoka Central Building, 1-7-1 Nishishinjuku, Shinjuku-ku, Tokyo 160, Japan
CANADA	Pergamon Press Canada, Suite 104, 150 Consumers Road, Willowdale, Ontario M2J 1P9, Canada

Copyright © 1986 Pergamon Books, Inc.

All rights reserved. No part of this publication may be reproduced, stored in a retrieval system or transmitted in any form or by any means: electronic, electrostatic, magnetic tape, mechanical, photocopying, recording or otherwise, without permission in writing from the publishers.

First printing 1986

Library of Congress Cataloging in Publication Data

Feindler, Eva L.
    Adolescent anger control.

    (Psychology practitioner guidebooks)
    Includes index.
    1. Anger. 2. Adolescent psychology.
3. Behavior therapy. 4. Cognitive therapy.
I. Ecton, Randolph B. II. Title. III. Series.
BF724.3.A55F45   1986   155.5   86-22601
ISBN 0-08-032374-X
ISBN 0-08-032373-1 (pbk.)

Printed in the United States of America

BF
724.3
.A55
F45
1986

I (E.L.F.) would like to dedicate this work to Ellie
Reese, who taught me to believe I could achieve, and
to Jessica, who gives me reasons to achieve.

DABNEY LANCASTER LIBRARY
LONGWOOD COLLEGE
FARMVILLE, VIRGINIA 23901

DABNEY LANCASTER LIBRARY

1000122311

Contents

List of Figures

List of Tables

Preface and Acknowledgments

Anger and aggressive behavior have long been identified as problems requiring both clinical and legal interventions. Adolescents who evidence difficulty in controlling their anger and often accompanying disruptive behaviors have been targets of numerous behavioral treatments. Problems with generalization of behavior change across settings, high recidivism rates and resistance to controlling contingencies have limited the effectiveness of traditional behavior modification programs. Rather than focus on the manipulation of consequences for aggressive behavior, we have developed a comprehensive self-management program designed to teach the adolescent to modify his own emotional arousal and behavior when faced with aversive or stressful situations.

The Adolescent Anger Control Program described in this guidebook is modeled after the important work of Ray Novaco and Don Meichenbaum. They have developed a stress inoculation or coping skills approach which incorporates a number of cognitive-behavioral techniques for arousal reduction and cognitive restructuring. We have blended these techniques with various self-control strategies known to be effective with children and adolescents (in particular, self-monitoring, self-evaluation and self-reinforcement) to facilitate the control of anger and aggression. Finally, we have included several social skills and assertion components in our program in order to facilitate prosocial responding. For these components as well as the training techniques of modeling and behavior rehearsal, we are indebted to Arnie Goldstein, his colleagues and their *Skill-streaming* approach.

The anger control program was implemented in the late 1970s with several adolescents residing at the Pressley Ridge School in Pittsburgh, Pennsylvania. A single-subject evaluation of the program indicated the effectiveness of this "package" with explosive adolescents and further research was planned. The bulk of our clinical endeavors has taken place at Sagamore Children's Center in Melville, Long Island, New York. We have refined the program, have incorporated the use of videotaping techniques and standardized symbolic modeling, and have concluded after running numerous group and individual sessions that the program is all inclusive. However, a certain amount of flexibility in the implementation of the program is possible and the specifics of each adolescent's treatment is individualized.

The anger control program described in this guidebook can be used on an individual or group basis in numerous settings. Adolescents involved in outpatient psychotherapy or in residential treatment or detention facilities can benefit. Further, caseworkers, probation counselors, special education teachers, guidance counselors, social workers, nurses, and psychologists may all find themselves at one time or another working with an angry adolescent without too many guidelines. We hope that this guidebook will help these professionals, and ultimately the adolescent, to effect change in the control of anger and aggression.

The first chapter contains an introduction to the area of anger and anger control interventions and a review of evaluative data. Chapter 2 provides detailed descriptions of behavioral assessment strategies useful for both clinical and research purposes. Chapters 3 and 4 contain the individual and group treatment manuals. These session-by-session descriptions of how to conduct the anger control program include: session objectives, training techniques, exercises, and homework assignments. The final chapters focus on clinical issues, difficulties and obstacles we have encountered and possible solutions, as well as extensions of anger control training.

We would like to thank all of the adolescents whom we have worked with over the years, especially those alumnae who have assisted in the running of groups. The entire staff of Sagamore Children's Center has been invaluable, in particular, Dr. Dennis Dubey, Debra Kingsley, and the childcare workers. Further, we must thank the graduate students of the Master's Degree Program in Applied Psychology at Adelphi University for their continued assistance as group leaders, data coders, and moral supporters throughout the years.

Specific to the preparation of this manuscript, we couldn't have done it without the unending editorial assistance of Judy Levey and Joan Feindler, and Patricia Carey's superb secretarial assistance. This guidebook is their labor of love for us.

And finally, we thank our families who instilled in each of us the belief that we could do it and who supplied the much needed encouragement all along.

Chapter 1
Introduction

BACKGROUND INFORMATION ON
ADOLESCENT BEHAVIOR PROBLEMS

Although adolescents comprise only 12% of the total U.S. population, the behavior problems exhibited by those between the ages of 13 and 18 are major ones. Crime is prevalent among adolescents. Juveniles account for 39% of all arrests for the index offenses of homicide, rape, robbery, aggravated assault, burglary, larceny, motor vehicle theft, and arson. Although the majority of all violent crimes has increased by 85% since 1960, the juvenile rate has increased by 233%, and between 1960 and 1979, the rate at which young people were arrested for all crimes increased by 95% (Empey, 1982). Not only is the incidence of crime increasing among adolescents, but the type of crime is more likely to be of an aggressive and violent nature (Stumphauzer, 1981).

Incidences of crime and delinquency are not the only forms of adolescent behavior that have drawn national attention. It has been estimated that 3.3 million teenagers between the ages of 14 and 17 (19% of this age group) could be classified as problem drinkers (Rachal, Maisto, Guess, & Hubbard, 1982) and that 93% have tried alcohol (Johnston, Bachman, & O'Malley, 1981). Further, 17% of adolescents are classified as current users of marijuana, and 65% report some illicit drug use (Johnston et al., 1981).

Behavior problems of the adolescent do not end here. Poor performance in school is estimated to occur in 25% of all school children, and 20% of U.S. adolescents fail to complete their high school education (Adelson, 1980). These high school dropouts then evidence higher rates of antisocial and addictive behaviors and are more apt to be unemployed. In addition, although more common among the adult population, suicide is the fourth leading cause of death among 15- to 19-year-olds, preceded only by accidents, homicide, and cancer (Adelson, 1980). Although it is often assumed that psychological interventions with adolescents experiencing such severe behavior problems are ineffective at best and that restrictive or punitive strategies must be implemented, there is literature to indicate that

1

cognitive-behavioral interventions with adolescents can bring about significant behavior change.

Although there are a variety of prevalent adolescent behavior problems, the most critical areas for intervention are those of anger and aggression. These problem behaviors interfere with the adolescent's adaptive functioning in school, in the family, or at work, and they strain the tolerance limits of those in authority positions. Frequently, the repeated performance of aggressive behaviors results in severe negative consequences from family and community systems. Furthermore, the repeated experience of intense anger may become overwhelming for the adolescent. Given this sequence, it is clear that clinical interventions for both internal anger arousal and the often accompanying aggressive behavior must be developed.

PROBLEM DEFINITION

Aggression and Anger

Aggression, according to behavioral theory, is a pattern of learned responses to both internal and external factors. It is maintained by such consequences as social reinforcement, relief from aversive stimulation, and acquisition of concrete rewards (Varley, 1984). There are numerous classifications of the different types of aggression, such as *instrumental* (responses performed in order to obtain specific outcomes) and *reactive* (a defensive response to real or perceived provocation). It has been theorized that reactive aggressive adolescents would be more likely to exhibit impulsive and anxious behavior and would be less likely to premeditate their aggressive acts, while instrumental aggressive adolescents would have longer histories of antisocial or delinquent behaviors and would be more deliberate in their attempt to secure desired outcomes (Lochman, 1984). The typologies of aggressive behavior, as well as the frequency and severity of their occurrence, vary widely in the adolescent population, but some aggressive behavior patterns seem quite stable over time. In a comprehensive review of 16 longitudinal studies of aggression in males from childhood through adulthood, Olweus (1979) found that aggressive persons maintained their relative ranking of aggression, as compared to their peers' behavior. This finding has spurred an increased interest in the prevention and control of aggression.

Anger has been defined by Novaco (1975, 1979) as an affective stress reaction to provocation events. Anger involves both physiological and cognitive determinants. It is mediated by the expectations an individual has regarding events, responses to these events, and by the appraisal of their meaning. Certainly, anger reactions need not be accompanied by aggressive behavior; however, with the impulsive adolescent population for whom this manual is designed, aggression often follows anger arousal. Indeed, in their now classic article, Rule and Nesdale (1976) review evidence consistent with the view that when a person's arousal state is anger, the anger acts as a determinant of aggression, which is directed primarily toward the goal of injuring the perceived source of anger. Research suggests that a person's anger and subsequent aggression can be increased or decreased depending upon that person's causal attribution of the physiological arousal experienced. Lochman, Burch, Curry, and Lampron (1984) use a cognitive-behavioral framework to conceptualize aggression as "a behavioral reaction due in part to distorted and inadequate cognitive processing of perceived provocations and frustrations" (p. 915).

Cognitive Appraisal Mechanisms

Beginning with Bandura (1973) and followed by Novaco (1979), the cognitive-behavioral theories of anger and aggression have emphasized the role of cognitive appraisal mechanisms. Ample research has demonstrated that the appraisal of events as provocation stimuli (direct or indirect threats, aversive stimuli, etc.) influences the magnitude of aggressive behavior. Aggressive adolescents have a tendency to believe that an interpersonal threat or provocation exists even when it may in fact not exist (Lochman, 1984). In fact, Nasby, Hayden, and DePaulo (1980) concluded from their research that boys rated as aggressive tended to perceive all filmed vignettes of anger, affection, dominance, and submission themes as reflecting hostility and dominance. Similarly, other researchers (Dodge & Frame, 1982; Forman, 1980) reported that aggressive children respond to hypothetical provocation incidents with significantly more irrational thoughts, aggressive statements, and negative evaluations than nonaggressive children. Further, Novaco's (1979) premise that anger is maintained and enhanced by the self-statements made by the individual in a provocation situation provides additional support for the primary role of cognitive processes in the generation of aggressive responses.

Cognitive Impulsivity and Mediation

A related set of cognitive skills that influence the occurrence of anger and aggression includes cognitive mediation strategies. Individuals who do not suffer from anger control problems employ a number of these cognitive processing skills to facilitate emotional arousal management. The first skill is the production of self-guiding verbalizations that help to inhibit automatic aggressive responding and prompt more adaptive responding. Research has indicated that these cognitive mediation strategies are deficient in aggressive children (Camp, 1977), who tend to respond more impulsively on cognitive tasks as well as during interpersonal interactions. These self-verbalizations are related to the characteristic response styles of children's conceptual tempo along the reflection-impulsivity dimension. Reflective children are more attentive, less aggressive, and are able to think of alternative responses to problem situations (Little & Kendall, 1979). Needless to say, adolescents who exhibit impulsive aggression have clear deficits in self-guiding speech.

The second skill is the ability to employ various problem-solving strategies. Spivack, Platt, and Shure (1976) have proposed that a set of discrete problem-solving skills (i.e., causal thinking, consequential thinking, means-end thinking, alternative thinking, and perspective taking) are essential to effective coping and social adjustment. These skills have been found to be deficient in hospitalized adolescents (Platt, Spivack, Altman, Altman, & Peizer, 1974) and delinquent populations (Gaffney & McFall, 1981; Little & Kendall, 1979).

Finally, there is the skill related to perspective taking, which emphasizes the ability to shift attention from a single aspect of an event and view other persons' perspectives. This functions as another cognitive mediation strategy that maximizes adaptive responding to interpersonal conflict situations and reduces the likelihood of aggressive responding. Research has indicated that delinquents have clear deficiencies in this area as well (Little & Kendall, 1979).

Arousal Management Skills

Since research has supported the conclusions that (a) general emotional arousal facilitates aggressive behavior, and (b) when emotional arousal is apparently labeled as anger, it leads to aggressive behavior (Rule & Nesdale, 1976), arousal management capability is a critical part of effective anger control. Indeed, one of the major components of Novaco's (1979) stress inoculation approach to anger treatment is the regulatory one—teaching the individual to regulate his/her own arousal. Skills training programs, whether involving social or self-management skills, are predicated on the individual's abilities to perform the skills and control interfering emotional arousal. Delinquent and aggressive adolescents may have numerous skills deficiencies, but they may also evidence performance deficits due to intense arousal, usually of anger or stress, during interpersonal conflict or frustrating situations.

There has been some positive evidence for systematic desensitization and relaxation strategies for individuals exhibiting anger disorders (Novaco, 1975; Warren & Mchellan, 1982). The notion of "desensitizing" emotional reactions to provoking stimuli parallels the stress inoculation approach, which teaches a variety of coping skills. Bornstein, Hamilton, and McFall (1981) suggest the development of treatment strategies designed to alleviate the anxiety component that often precedes defensive anger reactions (Novaco, 1979) and to reduce inhibitions surrounding the appropriate expression of anger in overcontrolled individuals who are prone to explosive violence. Although the relationship of physiological variables to the cognitive variables of the anger reaction is not clear (Moon & Eisler, 1983), anger arousal is an emotional state directly affecting the behavioral responses to either overt or misattributed provocation. Clearly, a successful anger and aggression management intervention must include the training of adaptive arousal management skills.

Summary

It is apparent that the cognitive-behavioral definitions of anger and aggression are complex. Indeed Lochman (1984) concludes that the "abilities to accurately appraise one's interpersonal situation, to inhibit impulsivity, to generate potential alternative behavioral responses, to anticipate external consequences for behaviors, to perceive responsibility and to handle associated anxiety . . . all clearly interact . . . to produce or to avoid aggressive behavior" (p. 37). These behavioral concepts, coupled with evidence against the curative effect of the catharsis hypothesis (Geen, Stonner, & Shope, 1975) validate the efforts to develop anger control procedures.

Traditional Behavioral Approaches to Aggression Control

Traditional behavioral approaches to the modification of aggressive behavior have been based on social learning theory, which defines aggression as a form of social behavior generated and maintained in much the same manner as other behaviors (Bornstein et al., 1981; Fehrenbach & Thelen, 1982). Aggressive behaviors are precipitated by several conditions, including provocation or aversive stimulation, high levels of emotional arousal (Rule & Nesdale, 1976), and anticipation of reinforcement or punishment contingencies. Consequent conditions, which serve to reinforce the acquisition and maintenance of aggressive behaviors, can also include the anticipated outcomes of not responding to provocation. However, the most powerful reinforcers for aggressive behaviors tend to be (a) the termination of the aversive stimulation or provocation, (b) attainment of the desired rewards or outcomes, and (c) social reinforcement, usually provided by peers (Bandura, 1973).

These factors, which serve to maintain and even strengthen aggressive behavior patterns, may be systematically manipulated to decrease the occurrence of aggression as well. Operant techniques, designed to control aggressive behaviors, have included extinction, which eliminates the reinforcing conditions maintaining the behavior, reinforcement for nonaggression and prosocial behavior, time out from positive reinforcement, response cost, and overcorrection, which requires repeated rehearsal of incompatible, positive behaviors (see Bornstein et al., 1981 and Goldstein, 1983 for review).

Although there have been numerous examples of the effectiveness of operant control techniques, the majority of these investigations have focused on retarded or schizophrenic populations in institutional settings. The effectiveness of external control techniques is maximized by the environmental control available in these settings. Bornstein et al. (1981) in their review of the modification of adult aggression conclude that the available literature does not address the comparative effectiveness of these operant techniques or their differential suitability for diverse patient populations and that the available data regarding maintenance of treatment gains is too limited to be of value. Finally, legal issues concerning the use of punishment and the withholding of amenities used as contingent rewards may curtail the implementation of operant procedures in institutional settings.

BEHAVIORAL INTERVENTIONS IN JUVENILE DELINQUENCY

Effectiveness of Contingency Management Interventions

In a review of behavioral interventions with delinquents in institutional settings, Blakely and Davidson (1984) note that token economy programs seem to be most prevalent and effective at improving specific academic, prosocial, and program behaviors. Token economy procedures have been used effectively in residential settings (Barkley, Hastings, Tousel, & Tousel, 1976; Hobbs & Holt, 1976; Kaufman & O'Leary, 1972) and group home settings (Fixsen, Phillips, & Wolf, 1972; Wood & Flynn, 1978).

Further, contingency management approaches have been employed in the successful reduction of aggression in the home (Patterson, 1975; Patterson, Reid, Jones, & Conger, 1975), inmate offenses (Bornstein, Rychtarik, McFall, Bridgewater, Guthuer, & Anton, 1980), and curfew violations (Alexander, Corbett, & Snigel, 1976). Moss and Rick (1981) presented a series of experiments based on token economy procedures with adolescent inpatients. Results indicated swift operant control over improvements in personal care behaviors; however, attendance and participation in group exercise and therapy were not effected. Further, attendance and participation in occupational therapy were affected positively by a combination of token reinforcement and time out (room restriction).

Reinforcement and response-cost contingencies, incorporated into a comprehensive program are effective in establishing prosocial and self-care skills, and in reducing disruptive and antisocial behaviors while the adolescent is in the program. However, there have been few reports of transfer and long-term maintenance of learned skills to natural environments. Moreover, upon closer inspection, these programs seem to have problems that limit the overall successfulness of their behavior change efforts.

Lack of Maintenance and Generalization

Much evidence indicates that behavior modification programs can be used to bring about changes in institutional behavior but that those changes will not generalize to improved behavior back in the community (Lane & Burchard, 1983). Appropriate school behavior, compliance to residential living requirements, reductions in antisocial or delinquent behaviors, and development of emotional control skills can be demonstrated in programs using clear reinforcements and punishment contingencies. However, unless specific generalization techniques are preplanned, the newly acquired behaviors soon fade when the adolescent is returned to the natural environment (Emshoff, Redd, & Davidson, 1976).

Lane and Burchard (1983) suggest that these behavior modification programs foster a dependency on contingencies that are too artificial and that the primary emphasis is on the development of compliance behavior through external reinforcement. These short-term changes do not seem to impact recidivism rates, poor academic achievement, or the probability of subsequent court contact (Blakely & Davidson, 1984; Burchard & Lane, 1984).

Competing Reinforcement Contingencies

Clearly, adolescents are by their very nature more attuned to peer reinforcement contingencies than those provided by authority figures in structured environments. Delinquent adolescents in particular seem to respond quickly and reliably to social reinforcement or avoidance of aversive stimuli provided by their peer group. If these contingencies are antagonistic to those contingencies designed to foster more appropriate responding, there will be less of a likelihood that the structured contingencies will be effective.

Lack of Powerful Reinforcers

Because of these rather strong peer reinforcement systems and due to the streetwise or "hardened" attitude of some aggressive adolescents, the behavior modifier may have a difficult time acquiring reinforcers strong enough to effect behavior change. Not all adolescents will respond to point systems or privilege rewards when illicit substances might be available from peers. Few institutional settings have the means *or* the desire to provide the types of reinforcers to which these adolescents might respond.

Low Frequency or Covert Behaviors

Aggressive and antisocial behaviors, for which many intervention programs could be designed, usually occur at a relatively low frequency and may be exhibited only when out of view of supervising adults. This makes it difficult to provide immediate consequences or to observe successive approximations of desired responses. The effectiveness of contingencies designed to impact these aggressive acts is thus limited by the rate and place of occurrence.

Inconsistencies of Behavior Change Agents

Varley (1984) indicates that the durability of change over time depends upon maintenance of positive changes by external agents outside the treatment setting. If these significant others fail to reinforce the changes the adolescent has made, there will be a gradual reduction in positive behaviors and a return of previously reinforced behavior patterns.

Developmental Influences

Finally, it would seem that the effectiveness of external reinforcement or punishment contingencies in a structured program would be impeded by certain adolescent developmental issues. Strivings toward autonomy and rebellion against authority, which are hallmarks of adolescence, seem in direct contradiction to the contingencies inherent in most behavior modification programs. Adolescents, especially aggressive and acting-out ones, do not take kindly to restrictions of their space and activities, nor to external control of tangible rewards. Point systems, token economies, time-out procedures, and the like, all require active structuring by external agents toward whom the adolescent may express anger and aggression (Varley, 1984). This may undermine the effectiveness of a well-designed behavior modification program.

Indeed, Lochman (1984) indicates that conflicts and aggression peak during middle adolescence. This may be related to adjustment to puberty and hormonal changes, the developmental tasks of individuation, separation from family, and/ or the increased stresses of adolescence (peer pressure, sexuality, school or job responsibilities). Since criticisms of behavioral approaches to the treatment of child and adolescent disorders have included the absence of a developmental focus (Phillips & Ray, 1980), it is important to recognize and incorporate developmental issues into treatment planning.

In summary, although there appears to be some success with behavior modification programs for aggressive adolescents, the long-term results are limited by several important factors (Wodarski, 1979). In fact, Stumphauzer (1981) indicates that difficulties in generalization planning as well as legal and ethical challenges to behavior modification have resulted in a decrease in contingency management programs in juvenile institutions. In his review of these programs, Varley (1984) concludes that a combination of approaches is needed. In a residential setting, the token economy with response-cost procedures is a good idea. However, much thought needs to be given to generalization issues. He suggests a gradual fading out of concrete reinforcers and a fading in of social reinforcers, as well as a move to intermittent schedules. Furthermore, the inclusion of self-management strategies is strongly recommended; this topic will be addressed in subsequent sections.

Alternative Interventions for Delinquent Adolescents

In response to these program shortcomings in traditional contingency management, programs incorporating additional intervention procedures have been developed. Of relevance to adolescents who exhibit aggressive behavior patterns and cognitive-behavioral skills deficiencies related to anger control are programs focused on contingency contracting with families, social skills training, and self-management training. These programs will be reviewed briefly as they relate to the anger control training program described in this manual.

Family Interventions and Contingency Contracting

In Burchard and Lane's (1984) review of systems-behavioral approaches to intervention in families with delinquent adolescents, the authors conclude that positive changes in family interaction are related to significant reductions in aversive child behavior, in postintervention offense rates on the part of delinquent adolescents and in sibling delinquent behavior recidivism. Further, although many families of behaviorally disordered adolescents are unwilling to participate in treatment, changes in family interactions are directly related to recidivism rates. Therefore, it seems critical to include parents in their adolescent's intervention program (Weathers & Liberman, 1975).

Kifer, Lewis, Green, and Phillips (1974) trained three parent-adolescent pairs in a negotiation process designed to improve communication, identification of issues, and generation of solutions. Following instructions, practice, and feedback about hypothetical conflict situations, there was an increase in agreements in the pairs, and these changes generalized to the home setting.

More recently, a comprehensive problem-solving communication training program for families with parent-adolescent conflict has been described by Robin and Foster (1984). The program includes stepwise problem-solving skills training, communication training, cognitive restructuring, and the changing of family structure and functions. Evaluations of this treatment package indicate problem-solving and communication skills acquisition, reductions in self-reported home conflicts, and maintenance of these gains over short-term intervals (Foster, Prinz, & O'Leary, in press; Robin, 1981). Although promising, these procedures were developed with young adolescents who were not necessarily exhibiting severe behavior problems nor residing in residential facilities. Thus, the application of problem-solving and communication training for families has yet to be investigated with explosive and aggressive adolescents.

Contingency contracting procedures extend the aforementioned reinforcement and response-cost techniques to include all family members. These techniques require some negotiation skills and the administration of rewards and punishments contingent upon each person's behaviors. Gross, Brigham, Hopper, and Bologna (1980) designed a behavioral contracting intervention with female adolescent delinquents and their parents as part of an overall program package that included a token economy, self-control, and social skills training. Parents and teachers alike reported a decrease in disruptive behaviors and truancy, and there was some improvement in academic functioning. Reciprocity counseling (Besalel & Azrin, 1981) incorporates positive communication training, self-correction, overcorrection, and positive practice techniques in a reciprocal fashion between family members. Initial effectiveness of this package was demonstrated with 12 adolescents who evidenced problems of chronic stealing, physical aggression, truancy, and lack of parental control. However, the lack of rigorous data collection and the reliance on self-reported data, limits the conclusions that can be drawn.

Social Skills Training Programs

Our focus on aggressive adolescents must include a brief look at the development of a variety of social skills training programs. The skills-deficit model of aggression postulates that aggressive behavior is a result of poor social skills that render a person incapable of expressing anger appropriately (Frederiksen & Eisler, 1977; Rahiam, LeFebvre, & Jenkins, 1980). Individuals who display abusive outbursts attempt to resolve conflicts through avoidance and by verbal and/or physical attacks that are rarely effective (Frederiksen, Jenkins, Foy, & Eisler, 1976). It has been suggested that adolescent offenders often behave maladaptively simply because they lack the requisite skills to act appropriately (Dishion, Loeber, Stouthamer-Loeber, & Patterson, 1984; Long & Sherer, 1984). Through the use of instructions, modeling, and behavior rehearsal a myriad of social skills designed to increase interpersonal effectiveness can be taught (Schinke, 1981). These programs seem directly relevant to the aggressive adolescent.

In a multiple baseline design across three behavior classes (interruptions, responses to negative communications, and requests for behavior change), Elder, Edelstein, and Narick (1979) evaluated a social skills training program for four hospitalized psychiatric adolescents. The data reported provide support for the treatment techniques of role play, modeling, coaching, and feedback. The measurement of generalization of improved social skills across environments indicated transfer of training. A similar social skills training program was developed for 76 young male offenders (Spence & Marzellier, 1981). Using modeling, role playing, feedback, social reinforcement, and task assignments, adolescents were taught a range of social and interpersonal skills. Although short-term gains involving basic skills were noted, follow-up and generalization data did not indicate transfer and maintenance of social skills.

Kolko, Dorsett, and Milan (1981) conducted a social skills training program with three hospitalized adolescents with various aggressive behavior patterns. Specific behaviors designated as anger control skills were trained via modeling, behavior rehearsal, and videotape feedback techniques. The multiple baseline evaluation across subjects and target skills indicated increases for all subjects in the percent of anger control skills used. Although this selection of anger control skills (including response latency of 3-6 seconds, oriented eye contact, neutral facial expression, moderate voice loudness, and assertive verbal response) was based on outcomes of previous training programs for aggressive clients, the relationship between these social skills and anger was not clear. Clearly, appropriate social skills are desirable alternatives to aggressive behavior. However, the authors note that the skills were not empirically derived (Kolko et al., 1981). Furthermore, there were no data available on actual aggressive behavior and therefore no data on increased anger control.

Although social skills training programs abound (Bornstein, Bellack, & Hersen, 1980; Collingswood & Genter, 1980; Filipczak, Archer, & Friedman, 1980; Goldstein, Sprafkin, Gershaw, & Klein, 1980; Long & Sherer, 1984; Ollendick & Hersen, 1979), there have been some criticisms of this approach. Freedman, Rosenthal, Donahoe, Schlundt, and McFall (1978) were critical of the emphasis on overall program evaluation. Fundamental issues, such as assessing individuals to determine whether they are actually deficient in the skills being taught and empirically establishing the content of the training programs, were ignored. Finally, there has been no robust demonstration that social skills training reduces aggressive behaviors of adolescents.

Of significance to the treatment of aggressive delinquent adolescents is a finding that particular types of juvenile offenders responded differently to treatment approaches. Long and Sherer (1984) evaluated a structured social skills training program (Goldstein et al., 1980) in 30 adolescent male offenders in a probation-counseling program. Following modeling, role play, and written assignment procedures, high frequency offenders were rated as more socially skillful, while low frequency offenders benefited more from a discussion control group. Further evidence from locus of control assessments indicated that social skills training supported the belief that one's behavior and consequences are controlled by oneself rather than by external factors. This finding suggests that self-control techniques, incorporated into skills training programs, may facilitate more socially acceptable behavior patterns.

Although there are sufficient data to support the hypothesis that there is a relationship between lack of competence in social situations and delinquent behavior, a causal relationship has not been established (Gaffney & McFall, 1981). In addition to deficiencies in the behavioral and cognitive skills needed to handle interpersonal situations, adolescents experiencing behavior problems have deficits in arousal management and impulse control skills. Goldstein, Glick, Zimmerman, Reiner, Coultry, and Gold (1985) recognized these complexities and developed a comprehensive intervention program for the acting-out adolescent: Aggression Replacement Training. This program includes: (a) a systematic, psychoeducational intervention designed to teach prosocial behaviors that can replace aggressive ones; (b) a moral education component designed to enhance actual, overt moral behavior, and (c) an anger control training component (Feindler, Ecton, Kingsley, & Dubey, 1986; Feindler & Fremouw, 1983; Feindler, Marriott, & Iwata, 1984b) designed to teach the inhibition of anger, aggression, and other forms of antisocial behavior. This component, directly modeled on our anger control manual, is hypothesized as a necessary adjunct to the social skills training, since anger and related affective states must be controlled before prosocial behaviors can be performed (Goldstein et al., 1985).

Self-Control Training with Adolescents

Introduction and Rationale

In general, self-control is viewed as the individual's governing of his/her own behavior to attain certain goals. This requires both the cognitive skills necessary to generate and evaluate response alternatives and the behavioral capacity to inhibit inappropriate responses and exhibit the desired responses (Little & Kendall, 1979). There has been an increased trend toward the development of self-control interventions for children and adolescents for several reasons. First, children who learn to control their own behavior and cope with frustration and the delay of gratification are better prepared to meet complex interpersonal and societal demands (Ollendick & Cerney, 1981). Secondly, behavior change agents are not always successful at implementing controlling contingencies; some behaviors are missed, and treatment becomes intermittent (O'Leary & Dubey, 1979; Ollendick & Cerney, 1981). Additionally, external behavior change agents may become discriminative cues for the performance of appropriate behaviors; when children or adolescents are in other stimulus settings, inappropriate behavior patterns may return. Finally, evidence suggests that controlling one's own behavior may lead to more efficient and durable behavior change both in classroom environments (Rosenbaum & Drabman, 1979) and other naturalistic settings (O'Leary & Dubey, 1979; Ollendick & Cerney, 1981).

In light of these issues, the developmental tasks confronting the maturing adolescent, and the nature of adolescent behavior problems (low frequency, high intensity, covert behaviors), self-control interventions seem most efficacious for adolescent treatment. Further, the aforementioned skills deficits, which are characteristic of delinquent adolescents (Kennedy, 1984) parallel self-control deficits. Kendall and Williams (1982) identify three types of self-management deficits:

1. Behavioral skill deficiencies: inability to perform self-observation, self-reinforcement, self-evaluation skills and to recognize cues to engage in self-management.
2. Cognitive deficiencies: poor discriminations, attributions, and problem solving responses which influence the acquisition, performance, and understanding of self-management skills.
3. Performance deficits: inability to exhibit requisite self-management skills because of high levels of interfering emotional arousal (may be anxiety, anger, or depression).

Self-Control Training with Delinquents

These skill deficits relate directly to the control of impulsive and aggressive behavior as well as to other target behaviors. Successful self-control intervention techniques must be incorporated into anger control treatment programs. There are numerous reports of successful self-control training programs with delinquent and/or aggressive adolescents. Case study reports indicate successful self-control treatment of an aggressive 16-year-old male in a high school setting (McCullough, Huntsinger, & Nay, 1977), and a preadolescent girl given to stealing (Stumphauzer, 1976).

Classroom Applications. Several larger investigations in adolescent school settings have been reported. Kaufman and O'Leary (1972) report the successful use of self-evaluation procedures within a classroom token program designed to decrease high rates of disruptive classroom behavior for 16 adolescents in a psychiatric residence. In a similar investigation of self-reinforcement and self-evaluation procedures, Santagrossi, O'Leary, Romanczyk, and Kaufman (1973) reported that self-evaluation procedures can be enhanced by self-determined reinforcement contingencies. However, these self-reinforcement strategies were only initially effective, and a matching procedure had to be instituted, whereby teacher determined contingencies were in control. It may be that self-management skills must be initially integrated with an already existing token economy program. External contingencies can then be faded out over time (Anderson, Fodor, & Alpert, 1976; Neilans & Israel, 1981).

Broad-Scope Programs. More recently, Brigham, Hopper, Hill, DeArmas, and Newsom (1985) developed a self-management training program that emphasizes concepts as well as specific behavioral techniques. Structured as an introductory laboratory course, 79 middle school students were taught how to analyze a situation, collect data, select an appropriate behavior change technique, and carry out the intervention. Results indicated a reduction in the number of school detentions received and an increase in knowledge of behavioral principles and problem solving. The authors suggested that the teaching of concepts or rules may contribute to the transfer and maintenance of behavior change. This type of broad scope behavioral training program was based on earlier work by Gross et al. (1980) with predelinquent youth in the community. In all examples, subjects conducted successful behavior change projects. However, there was no real assessment of actual application of principles to other problems. Although the population used in these investigations evidenced only mild disruptive behavior patterns, the success of the self-management focus supports the extension of these procedures to adolescents exhibiting anger and aggressive behaviors.

Cognitive Self-Control Strategies. Snyder and White (1979) incorporated self-instructional training, a more cognitive-behavioral strategy, into their treatment of delinquent adolescents. Fifteen adolescents who were in a residential treatment center due to severe behavior problems (aggression, drug use, criminal activities, etc.) received training in the use of self-verbalizations to control inappropriate behavior. Self-statements designed to inhibit impulsive and aggressive behaviors and to prompt more adaptive responses to interpersonal situations were modeled and rehearsed. The self-instructional training group demonstrated significant improvement in the performance of daily living requirements (school attendance and completion of social/self-care responsibilities) and a decrease in observed impulsive behaviors, as compared to a control group of delinquents.

It seems that this type of cognitive restructuring is a necessary component of self-control training with adolescents. In fact, Camp (1977) indicates that maintaining response inhibition on both impersonal and interpersonal tasks depends upon an effective linguistic control system.

Further, Little and Kendall (1979) conclude that an adolescent will exhibit self-controlled behavior to the extent that he/she possesses a response repertoire containing the necessary cognitive and behavioral skills and is motivated to use them in a particular situation. In their review of behavioral treatment of adolescent delinquents, Lane and Burchard (1983) highlight the need to develop programs that shape decision making, self-control, and problem solving. They assert that "students should be involved in setting personal objectives, self-evaluation, problem solving, and other more internally controlled cognitive activities rather than being the passive participants of externally controlled [contingencies]" (p. 367).

Self-Control of Anger and Aggressive Behavior. Although there have been presentations of the effectiveness of behavior modification techniques for reduction of aggressive behavior (Patterson, 1975), the cognitive-behavioral approach to the treatment of anger and aggression has become the dominant one (Wilson, 1984). Novaco (1975) pioneered a coping skills approach to the treatment of chronic anger problems in adults. Using Meichenbaum's (1975) stress inoculation approach, Novaco trained clients in the use of:

1. cognitive mediation techniques (attentional focus strategies, cognitive restructuring, problem-solving skills, and self-instructions)
2. arousal reduction methods (primarily relaxation and counterconditioning)

Central to the effectiveness of this treatment package is the combination of educational and application procedures in which clients practice these anger control methods in *in vivo* stressful situations. This helps to promote transfer and generalization of newly acquired skills and desensitize the client to stressful and/or anger provoking stimuli. These anger control skills were successfully trained in a hospitalized patient with severe anger problems (Novaco, 1977a), police officers (Novaco, 1977b), probation counselors (Novaco, 1980), and adults at risk for cardiovascular disorders (Novaco, 1985).

Also critical in the development of anger control treatments is the work of Camp (1977). Based upon her conclusions that young aggressive boys failed to use covert verbal mediation, Camp, Blum, Hebert, and van Doornick (1977) developed a "think-aloud" cognitive-behavioral program for impulsive, aggressive boys. The program was designed to address the appropriate content of self-statements and promote spontaneous use of self-guiding speech when confronted with both social and cognitive problems. Designed as a psychoeducational training program that could be carried out by teachers, the content of the programs, described by Camp and Ray (1984) is presented in Table 1.1.

This self-instructional program, which incorporates cognitive modeling and interpersonal problem-solving components, resulted in increases in prosocial and problem-solving behavior and decreases in aggressive behaviors in young boys. Although this program was designed for young children and does not explicitly focus on the arousal of anger, the program objectives and methods complement those of Novaco's (1975) anger management training and together form the basis for the adolescent anger control program described in this manual. Before embarking on a detailed description of the anger control training package and the research findings in support of the efficacy of the program, a brief look at the primary self-control strategies is necessary.

Self-Instruction Component

The primary component of both the stress inoculation and the "think-aloud" approach is the use of self-instructions. Originated as a therapy technique by Meichenbaum and Goodman (1971), self-instructions are designed to train impulsive individuals to provide themselves with internally generated verbal commands or guiding statements, to respond to these instructions appropriately, and to strengthen the mediational properties of their own inner speech (Bornstein, 1985). Self-instructions are designed to help alter the antecedents that are presumed to affect the occurrence of undesirable responses (Sanders, 1978). However, with regard to anger control, the self-instructions or coping statements generated to facilitate anger control (i.e., "Calm down," "Don't take it personally," etc.) must be congruent with an adaptive appraisal of aversive events and appropriate expectations of response to provocation (Novaco, 1979). In fact, Novaco (1979) has suggested viewing a provocation in terms of sequential stages and generating self-guiding verbalizations for each stage.

Table 1.1. The Think-Aloud Program

Treatment Objectives of the Think-Aloud Program Are:
1. Use verbalizations to inhibit first responses in a problem situation
2. Develop an organized approach to problem solving
3. Increase the repertoire of alternative response solutions
4. Develop a language for understanding cause and effect
5. Develop a repertoire of evaluation skills
6. Use both cognitive/impersonal problems and social/interpersonal problems to teach cognitive skills

Treatment Elements of the Think-Aloud Program Are:
1. Adult modeling of cognitions
2. Stimulating overt verbalizations of child's thoughts, followed by fading to covert levels
3. Promoting independence in the use of these skills
4. Promoting generalization by applying the skills to many contexts
5. Providing verbal transitions to promote generalizations to real-life situations

---

Table 1.2. Self-Statements for Coping with Anger Arousal

---

1. Preparing for conflict/provocation:
   "I'll be able to handle this; I'm prepared."
   "I won't take it personally."
   "This could get rough, but I know what to say."
2. Impact and confrontation:
   "Just stay calm."
   "There's no point in blowing up."
   "I'm in control of myself."
   "Just think of what I have to do."
3. Coping with arousal:
   "Just relax and take a deep breath."
   "I feel my heart pumping; time to slow down."
   "Reduce the tension, and take things step-by-step."

As can be seen by the list in Table 1.2 of potential self-statements to use in anger control, self-instructions focus not only on arousal management and cognitive reappraisal, but also on problem solving and impulse delay. Copeland (1982; Copeland & Hammel, 1981) provides an excellent review of the various individual factors that influence the outcome of self-instructional training with children. There are age, cognitive functioning, and motivational issues that may determine both the content of effective self-instructions and the training format. These developmental changes in cognitive functioning have been previously documented (Barenborm, 1977; Santostefano & Rieder, 1984). Further, research has indicated that training in general, problem-solving oriented self-instruction, rather than specific, task focused instruction, may promote the transfer and maintenance of self-control behaviors (Kendall & Braswell, 1982; Schlesser, Meyers, & Cohen, 1981). Effective coping in relation to provocation and anger arousal requires flexibility in the cognitive structuring and the mediated responses to stimuli that have previously elicited anger (Novaco, 1979). Finally, the effectiveness of self-instructions is related to reinforcement of appropriate self-verbalizations, actual *in vivo* use of the instructions, and key individual differences in subjects (Copeland 1982, 1981). These variables must be kept in mind in the development of effective self-management programs.

Self-Assessment Component

The therapeutic model proposed by Novaco and integrated into this anger control manual stipulates that anger arousal is an emotional response to stressful and/or aversive stimuli and must be reconceptualized as a signal to implement adaptive coping strategies. This requires an extensive analysis of the individual's anger reactions (including cognitive, physiological, and motoric components) and internal and external antecedents to anger. The procedures of self-observation and self-monitoring help to facilitate recognition of the components of the anger reaction sequence and pave the way for successful implementation of anger control methods. Self-monitoring is a complex pattern of behavior and involves the discrimination between overt and covert antecedent stimuli, the subsequent responses and consequences of responding, and the actual recording of these variables. The procedure itself may function to enhance the skills of problem identification and the recognition of operating behavioral contingencies (Heppner, 1978). Factors that may influence the accuracy of self-monitoring were identified in an investigation of the self-recording of cleaning behaviors of young adolescents (Lyman, Rickard, & Elder, 1975). These factors (i.e., contingent reinforcement of self-recording, awareness of reliability checks, and overt verification of data) must be incorporated into any effective self-control program.

Self-Evaluation Component

Providing oneself with feedback on the performance of both cognitive and behavioral responses to situations serves to enhance skills acquisition and maintenance. The identification of successful coping responses, which involves the discrimination of antecedent stimuli and target responses and the evaluation of these responses according to some specific criteria, may act as a cue for self-reinforcement (Heppner, 1978). The inclusion of self-evaluation skills in a training program can enhance the probability of reinforcement of newly acquired self-control skills.

The effectiveness of self-evaluation skills is determined by the accuracy of self-monitoring and self-reinforcement, which seem to depend on clearly specified behaviors and well-defined criteria for success (Akamatsu & Farudi, 1978; Sanders, 1978). Extensive demonstration and rehearsal of the requisite skills for self-evaluation are necessary and can be easily incorporated into the self-instructional training. In fact, Novaco (1979) includes an additional stage for self-instructional control of anger:

Subsequent Reflection
(a) When conflict is unresolved:
    —"I tried my best, but I'm not going to continue to be upset."
(b) When conflict is resolved:
    —"I did a great job controlling myself."
    —"I accomplished my goal without getting angry."
    —"I handled that pretty well."

These reflective self-statements approximate self-reinforcement since they serve a performance feedback function and increase the probability of subsequent performance of anger control skills. Indeed, Lochman et al. (1984) report that their anger coping treatment for aggressive boys was enhanced by a goal setting and reinforcement strategy. This may have prompted spontaneous self-reinforcement and corrective feedback responses. With adolescents, self-reinforcement statements may occur in the absence of the target behavior or may reflect very lenient performance criteria. But if our treatment focus is on the self-control of angry and aggressive behaviors, accurate and meaningful self-evaluation skills can be shaped and prompted throughout the anger control program.

Arousal Management Component

In addition to regulating cognitions and initiating various self-control/problem-solving responses, regulation of physical arousal surrounding provocation is a major component of anger control training (Novaco, 1979). Relaxation training can help to identify internal cues associated with the tension accompanying anger arousal and can serve as an alternative response to provocation stimuli. However, Novaco (1979) notes that the therapeutic objective is to develop a sense of self-control over physiological arousal rather than to countercondition a relaxation response to aversive stimuli. Decreases in physiological arousal via relaxation methods (Elitzur, 1976), deep breathing, and imagery (Garrison & Stolberg, 1983) enhance the individual's cognitive restructuring and subsequent anger control.

Adaptive Skills Development

In addition to developing more adaptive cognitive appraisals, self-guiding verbalizations, and arousal management skills, anger control training must assist the individual to develop overt coping skills. These skills, taught via modeling and behavior rehearsal, help the individual to express anger in more appropriate ways and to improve problem solving and interpersonal communications. Traditionally this has included a focus on remediation of social skills deficiencies (Fredericksen et al., 1976; Gaffney & McFall, 1981; Sprafkin, Gershaw, & Klein, 1980; Rahaim et al., 1980), assertion training (Lee, Hallberg, & Hassard, 1979), and problem solving (D'Zurilla & Goldfried, 1971). The anger control program described in this manual includes skills training in each of these areas as they relate to successful resolution of provocation incidents. The program is designed to teach the adolescent to assess each anger-provoking situation and to implement the most effective response from his/her repertoire of anger control responses. These behavioral responses are then evaluated according to their effectiveness in terms of both anger management and problem resolution.

Evaluation of Anger Control Interventions with Adolescents

Although there are numerous reports attesting to the effectiveness of anger control training with adults (see Novaco, 1979, 1985 for review) and aggressive children (Camp et al., 1977; Henshaw, Henker, & Whalen, 1984; Lochman, Nelson, & Sims, 1981; Lochman et al., 1984; Robin, Schneider, & Dolnick, 1976; Saylor, Benson, & Einhaus, 1985), there have been only a few investigations with adolescents.

Building on a series of successful case studies employing aspects of anger control methodology (Bistline & Frieden, 1984; Hamberger & Lohr, 1980; Kaufmann & Wagner, 1972; McCullough et al., 1977; Quick, Francis, Hernandez, & Freedman, 1980) Feindler and her colleagues extended effective anger techniques to populations of aggressive adolescents. In an initial study (Feindler, 1979), self-monitoring and anger management strategies (in particular self-instructions, self-evaluation, problem solving, and arousal reduction skills) were presented in individual training sessions to four court adjudicated adolescents at a residential treatment facility. Employing a multiple baseline design across four subjects and four matched comparison subjects, Feindler obtained self-reports, ratings by others, and direct observation data on all subjects. Figure 1.1 presents the data from direct observations conducted in both the classroom and cottage environments.

Although there was considerable intersubject as well as intrasubject variability, results indicated reductions in observed aggressive behaviors for all subjects from baseline to anger control training, with little effect evidenced for the self-monitoring of anger provocations alone. Further analyses (see Figure 1.2) indicated changes in some categories of aggressive behavior and not in others. This may indicate a need for a comprehensive initial analysis of the adolescent's anger reactions and the tailoring of the anger control program to the specific behavioral responses of the individual.

Next, the anger control training program was redeveloped as a group intervention and evaluated in an in-school junior high school program for multisuspended and delinquent youth (Feindler, Marriott, & Iwata, 1984b). Eighteen randomly selected students received biweekly anger control training for a total of 14 sessions, and another sample of 18 students served as the comparison group. A school-based contingency management program designed to improve academic behaviors and control disruptive and aggressive behaviors was in effect for all students during the course of the study. Figure 1.3 presents the evaluation data for both groups across the baseline, training, and follow-up phases of the study. Compared to the comparison group, students receiving anger control training showed some decreases in the mean rates of fines received via the contingency management program for mild (single fines) and severe (double fines) categories of aggressive and disruptive behaviors. Further data from pre- and post-self-report assessments indicated improvements in problem-solving abilities, cognitive reflectivity, and teacher rated checklists of impulsivity. Anecdotal evidence indicated that the group intervention approach (three groups of six adolescents each) was quite effective, since *in vivo* provocations often occurred, and adaptive responses could be immediately reinforced.

The group anger control training program was then extended to an adolescent population evidencing more severe behavior problems; namely, aggressive adolescents in an inpatient psychiatric facility (Feindler et al., 1986). Adolescents ranging in age from 13 to 16 years comprised the treatment group ($N=8$), the waiting list control group ($N=8$ subjects from a different unit), and a within-unit control

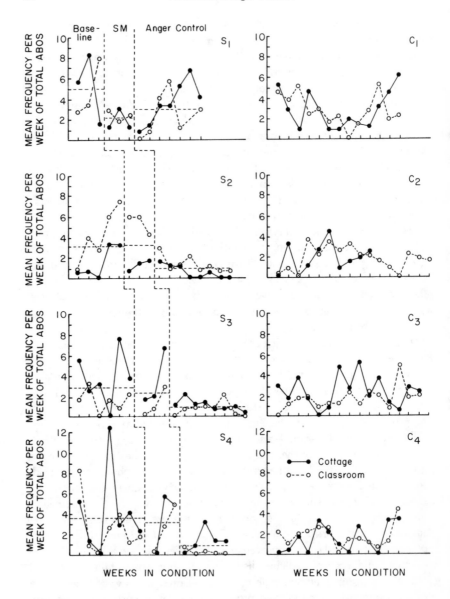

FIGURE 1.1. Multiple Baseline Evaluation of Anger Control Training. *Note.* From "Stress Inoculation Training for Adolescent Anger Problems," by E. L. Feindler and W. J. Fremouw. In D. Meichenbaum and M. E. Jaremko (Eds.), *Stress Reduction and Prevention*, 1983, (p. 474). Copyright 1983 by Plenum Publishing Corp. Used with permission.

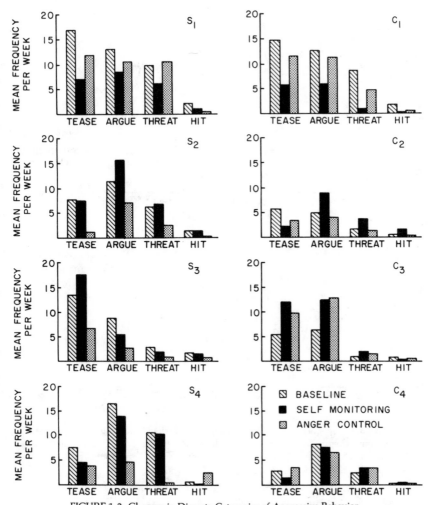

FIGURE 1.2. Changes in Discrete Categories of Aggressive Behavior

group ($N=8$ subjects who were new admissions to the treatment unit). All adolescents in this facility participated in a contingency management program employing levels of response-cost punishments. Bedroom restrictions were a result of
physical aggression toward others, and unit restrictions were a result of rule violations due to disruptive and noncompliant behavior. Figure 1.4 presents these
response-cost data across baseline, treatment, and follow-up phases.

The results indicate that the 11-week anger control training was effective in
reducing aggressive and disruptive behaviors. Further, data from pre- and post-
measures indicated improvements in self-control, as rated by teachers and direct-
care staff, in problem-solving abilities, and in social skills. Social skillfulness was

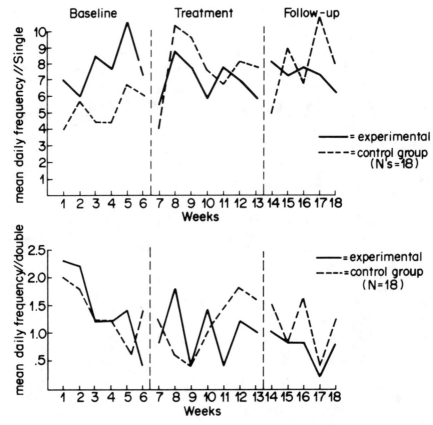

FIGURE 1.3. Group Anger Control for Delinquent Junior High School Students. *Note.* From "Group Anger Control Training for Junior High School Delinquents" by E. L. Feindler, S. A. Marriott, and M. Iwata, 1984, *Cognitive Therapy and Research, 8,* p. 306. Copyright 1984 by Plenum Publishing Corp. Used with permission.

assessed during standardized videotaped interactions with a confederate at a pre- and posttraining. Decreases in hostile verbalizations and aggressive responses, as well as increases in eye contact, appropriate requests for behavior change and in the use of discrete assertive and anger control responses were noted. Finally, anecdotal follow-up data indicated that 90% of adolescents receiving anger control training in an expanded institutional program were able to make successful transitions to community living arrangements or to their families. These successful results with an inpatient psychiatric population contradict the negative findings found by Saylor, Benson, and Einhaus (1985), but this may reflect our inclusion of an assertion and social skills component geared to teach more adaptive responses to frustration and general problem-solving training.

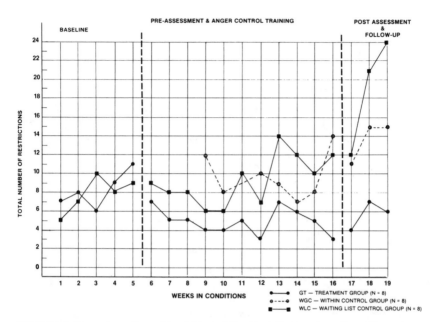

FIGURE 1.4. Group Anger Control for Adolescent Psychiatric Patients. *Note.* From "Group Anger-Control Training for Institutionalized Psychiatric Male Adolescents" by E. L. Feindler, R. B. Ecton, D. Kingsley, and D. Dubey, 1986, *Behavior Therapy, 17,* p. 119. Copyright 1986 by Association for Advancement of Behavior Therapy. Used with permission.

Several other authors have developed anger control intervention packages for use with aggressive adolescents as well. As mentioned previously, Snyder and White (1979) and Williams and Akamatsu (1978) conducted successful self-instruction training programs with delinquent adolescents. Snyder and White (1979) reported reductions in disruptive/impulsive behaviors. However, due to the lack of reliable and comprehensive direct observation and paper-pencil measures, the generalizability of these results is limited. In the Williams and Akamatsu (1978) study, delinquents showed improved performance on impersonal cognitive tasks, but the attention control group improved as well. Further, neither of these studies directly targeted aggressive or explosive behavior or interpersonal conflict for intervention.

Schlichter and Horan (1981) presented a stress inoculation program to institutionalized male delinquents evidencing verbal and physical aggression. Court adjudicated adolescents assigned to the stress inoculation condition attended weekly sessions in which anger coping skills (self-instructions, relaxation, assertive responding, and self-reinforcement) were modeled and rehearsed. Compared to subjects receiving relaxation training alone and subjects receiving no treatment, the adolescents trained in anger management showed improvements in role-played provocations. Unfortunately, the anger control training had no effect on verbal aggression, physical aggression, or global adjustment in the naturalistic setting. Although the authors cite factors particular to institutional settings that mitigate against generalized treatment effects and indicate inadequacies in data collection procedures, the stress inoculation approach to anger management can be effective.

Finally, perhaps the most comprehensive skills training program developed for adolescents, entitled Aggression Replacement Training, was reported by Goldstein et al. (1978, 1985). This intervention program includes three components:

1. *Behavior facilitation:* A psychological phase in which 50 prosocial skills are trained as alternative responses to aggression.

2. *Aggression and anger inhibition:* Cognitive skills training based on Feindler's (1979; Feindler et al., 1984b, & Feindler et al., 1986) anger control program. Identification of anger-eliciting cues, self-statement disruption training, and refocusing anticipation of consequences are some of the skills taught as alternative, inhibiting responses to provocation.

3. *Moral education:* Presentation and discussion of moral dilemmas designed to enhance the likelihood that the adolescent will choose to respond to the world more prosocially. This cognitive component provides constructive directionality toward prosocialness and away from antisocialness (Goldstein et al., 1985).

The comprehensiveness of this multimodal program is noteworthy, and the results from an ongoing evaluation of 60 incarcerated adolescents in group training are encouraging. Certainly, this triple-component approach addresses issues raised earlier vis à vis the relationship of social skills training to management of anger and aggressive behavior. The combination of inhibiting responses, adaptive prosocial responses, and moral choices makes theoretical sense and ameliorates the various skill deficiencies in delinquent populations. Unfortunately, there are no available research evaluations to date in which objective and reliable pre–post and continuous assessment strategies have been incorporated.

There is little doubt that the cognitive-behavioral skills taught to clients in the stress inoculation, anger control programs serve to control aggressive behavior and/or provocations and facilitate more appropriate social and problem-solving skills. There have been numerous case study applications as well as group interventions documenting improvements in role-play performances, perceptions of greater self-control made by significant others, and ward behavior. The anger control methodology works with aggressive adolescents. Moreover, variations in the training environment are easily incorporated into individual differences in the adolescent's behavior patterns.

To date, there have been limited data available on the comparison of various anger control techniques. It is obvious that not all adolescents need all skills in the same format. Component analysis research as well as comprehensive individual assessments will aid in the development of the optimum client-treatment match. Interestingly, Moon and Eisler (1983) compared the effectiveness of three behavioral treatment strategies with an attention-control group in the reduction of anger in male undergraduates. Following random assignment to either a cognitive stress inoculation group, a problem-solving group, a social skills group, or a minimal attention group, data were collected from self-reports of anger, role-played anger provocations, and self-monitoring of real life anger-provoking situations. Results indicated that the problem-solving and social skills training both reduced anger-provoking cognitions and increased socially skilled behaviors, whereas the stress inoculation training resulted only in a reduction of anger related cognitions. These data, although not from a clinical sample of aggressive or hospitalized adolescents, support the recommendations of Goldstein et al. (1985) for multicomponent treatments.

The remainder of this book will present both an individual and group approach to anger control training. Following the chapter on assessment of anger control and evaluations of training programs, guidelines and session-by-session descriptions for individual training and the Art of Self-Control Group approach will be presented. Factors influencing successful and unsuccessful outcomes for these programs will be covered in chapter 5. Finally, chapter 6 will provide a program review and suggestions for new applications of anger control training methods.

Chapter 2

Assessment and
Evaluation Methods

DIAGNOSTIC DECISIONS

It is still difficult to determine exactly which types of angry and aggressive adolescents will benefit the most from the cognitive-behavioral anger control training program. There are limited data on the treatment efficacy for various clinical subtypes, so many of the recommendations for inclusion in the training program are made by hunch. However, a review of diagnostic characteristics typical of aggressive adolescents can form the basis for selection of adolescents for the program.

DSM-III Categories

A review of the adolescents who have successfully completed the anger control training program in both inpatient and outpatient settings indicates that certain diagnostic categories are clearly represented. Most of the adolescents had a clinical diagnosis of Conduct Disorder—Aggressive Type. The subclassification of either unsocialized or socialized was equally distributed. Adolescents receiving this diagnosis must display a repetitive and persistent pattern of aggressive conduct in which the basic rights of others are violated for at least 6 months. In numerous cases, however, the adolescent has infrequently exhibited such severely aggressive behavior and has instead displayed less aggressive behavior (perhaps verbal threats or mild physical provocations) on a continuous basis.

The next most represented diagnostic category is that of Oppositional Disorder, in which the adolescent must display a pattern of disobedient, negativistic, and provocative opposition to authority figures for at least 6 months (*DSM-III*, 1980). This pattern can be manifested by violations of minor rules or stubbornness and is seen more often in our younger samples and in outpatient or school settings.

Other diagnoses have included Attention Deficit Disorder, which is characterized by inattention, impulsivity, and hyperactivity, Intermittent Explosive Disorder, characterized by discrete episodes of loss of control of aggressive impulses resulting in assault or destruction of property, and Antisocial Personality Disorder. This last category includes a history of truancy, delinquency, running away, persistent lying, and other antisocial acts, but is reserved for adolescents of at least 18 years of age.

Adolescents with all of the above clinical diagnoses may benefit from the anger control training program depending on some of the other factors described below. Given the individualized approach to the analysis of the adolescent anger provocation behaviors and the smorgasbord of control techniques taught, the effectiveness of the program does not rest on selecting adolescents based only on their clinical diagnoses.

Cognitive Functioning

Since many of the anger control techniques require changes in cognitive appraisal of precipitating events, self-guiding verbalizations, and self-observation and evaluation, the adolescent's level of cognitive functioning is important. The self-control skills taught must be encoded, stored in memory, accessed, and implemented at the appropriate time during an anger provocation. All of this requires cognitive abilities in the normal or near normal intellectual range. Most of the adolescents who have successfully completed the program have had a measured IQ of 90 or above. However, if external contingencies of reinforcement are placed on learning and performing the more observable anger control skills, adolescents with borderline or mild retardation levels might benefit. However, with a lower functioning adolescent, it is recommended that the program be broken down into smaller steps and taught on a one-to-one basis.

Behavior Problem History

Clearly, the main reason for referral to an anger control training program is an adolescent's pattern of acting out or aggressive behavior, usually accompanied by heightened emotional arousal expressed as intense anger. It is therefore important to analyze the adolescent's anger problem history during a screening process and separate these explosive incidents from the usual histories of antisocial acts such as lying, stealing, and the like. Adolescents who have been classified as juvenile delinquents, probably based on court contact, do not necessarily benefit from this program unless their inappropriate acts are precipitated by uncontrolled anger outbursts or are correlated with anger and aggression arousal.

There are numerous data available to indicate that there are different types of aggressive behavior patterns, although most remain stable over the course of the adolescent's life (Olweus, 1980). Lochman (1984) reviews several of the factor analytic studies done to clarify the characteristics that make up each of these types. For our clinical screening purposes, it is helpful to evaluate the adolescent's history along two dimensions: internalizing versus externalizing, and trait versus reactive. The first dimension refers to the expression of anger and the target of that expression. Some adolescents act out their anger, with persons or property serving as targets, while others direct their anger at themselves and inhibit most of the aggressive responses. Those externalizing adolescents will need to learn to identify the emotional and cognitive mediators of aggression and preempt the direct expression of the anger. The internalizing adolescent, however, will present more depressive symptomatology and will need emphasis on cognitive restructuring and the appropriate expression of anger. Further, adolescents who are highly reactive to anger provocations and appear to be quite impulsive in their aggression seem more appropriate for the anger control training than those who have a long history of carefully planned aggressive acts with the intent to harm. These adolescents are more resistant to this cognitive-behavioral program and most often do *not* have a self-control problem.

Finally, the actual topography, frequency, and intensity of the responses that accompany the adolescent's anger outburst must be analyzed during the treatment selection process. In order to shape the anger control skills, the adolescent will require *in vivo* practice in self-control. This means that the adolescent whose history includes frequent temper outbursts of a mild to moderate intensity will have frequent practice incidents. An adolescent who evidences rare, violent outbursts requiring physical isolation or restriction will have fewer practice incidents and many more external contingencies placed upon his/her behavior. In terms of topography, the aggressive responses may range from mild teasing to verbal threats, hitting/kicking, or property damage. What is of most importance, however, is the anger arousal that precedes and usually accompanies the aggressive responses. This is the main focus of this intervention program and therefore must be a part of the adolescent's repertoire. Adolescents who reportedly experience no anger arousal may not be aware of the cognitive and physiological responses and may require some pretraining.

Contraindications

There are some behavior patterns that may interfere with the anger control training. Adolescents experiencing extreme depression and/or suicidal thoughts (perhaps the extreme form of the internalizing characteristic) may not have the motivation or desire to participate in the treatment or complete any of the assigned tasks. This, along with the rather severe cognitive distortions that accompany depression, will certainly interfere with treatment.

Adolescents who are current substance abusers pose additional problems, since their intoxicated state will interfere in the treatment process, especially in the group format. They will also have lower motivation and commitment to carry out tasks and will experience difficulty with the auditory memory and sequencing skills required for the cognitive restructuring component. The substance abuse pattern must be targeted for intervention prior to any anger control intervention.

Finally, those adolescents who have thought disorders or delusions will also be unable to benefit fully from the program. Even though separate components of the package can be trained, the cognitive restructuring sections will be difficult to comprehend and incorporate for those with psychotic behavior patterns.

Summary

Adolescents who have a history of reactive and impulsive aggression, manifested by mild to moderate forms of aggression in response to frustration and anger arousal will benefit most from this program. Average intellectual functioning, few episodes of severe, deliberate antisocial acts, and a lack of psychiatric contraindications are also desirable characteristics to screen for. Finally, when planning the composition of training groups, the more homogeneous the adolescent sample, the better.

ASSESSMENT DEVICES

The primary focus of this chapter is to provide an overview of the various types of assessment methods that can be used to screen and evaluate adolescents for anger control training. A description of each method is presented along with a detailed discussion of how to best obtain reliable data on adolescents' aggressive behavior patterns. Issues of practicality and usefulness of each assessment method are highlighted.

Self-Monitoring Procedures

Introduction

The cognitive-behavioral model of anger management proposes several component responses exhibited by the target individual during an anger provocation. These include physiological, cognitive, and overt motoric responses that may form an aggression sequence. Physiological arousal, usually an individual pattern of stress responses, may include flushed face, sweaty palms, racing heart, and the like. Accompanying cognitive responses may include faulty attributions of blame, misperceptions, negative self-statements, aggression-inducing self-talk, and so forth.

The manner in which these covert responses present themselves during an anger provocation (namely, eliciting stimuli, intensity, and topography of discrete responses and their patterns) are necessary for a fine-tuned analysis of the adolescent's anger response chain. If a comprehensive assessment of these factors is not completed, the particular anger control strategies contained in the program cannot be matched to the individual's behavior patterns. Therefore, an assessment of these covert physiological and cognitive factors must precede training and accompany training components in order to provide the adolescent with feedback.

While the overt motoric components of an anger provocation incident are observable to trained data collectors or others in the adolescent's environment, these covert responses must be assessed in an indirect fashion. Self-monitoring, which requires that the clients themselves observe and record occurrences of their own behavior, appears for several reasons to be the best technique for collecting these types of data.

1. The adolescent is the one person who is always present during the anger provocations! Therefore, although there are clearly strong biases and distortions affecting the collection by the adolescent of data on his/her own behavior, the continual nature of self-monitoring will provide the most comprehensive assessment in the long run.

2. The only way to access covert events (both physiological arousal and discrete cognitive responses) is through some form of self-recording. Since it is crucial to monitor these events, this method seems necessary.

3. Self-monitoring, although primarily an assessment device, serves therapeutic functions as well. The actual recording of data during an anger provocation (or shortly thereafter) provides the angry adolescent with a new response, one that may prevent the immediate escalation of an incident. Further, the process of analyzing the anger incident into its component parts, through completion of the self-monitoring data sheet, provides the adolescent with a behavioral framework for understanding and changing his/her behavior. This also helps to teach the adolescent the concepts and vocabulary comprising the cognitive-behavioral model of anger management. Finally, the actual self-monitoring technology (data sheets, recording notebooks, etc.) serves as a discriminative stimulus for anger control responses in each stimulus situation where the adolescent records his/her behavior. This simple cuing device assists in the transfer of newly acquired control skills to extra-therapeutic environments.

4. Self-monitoring assessment procedures allow the adolescent to report his/her side of a particular anger incident and express freely all of the details of the incident. Regardless of the outcome, the adolescent can justify his/her own responses and can also learn to evaluate his/her own behavior. This not only offers the clinician a rich data source, but undercuts much of the adolescent resistance to completing a paper and pencil task.

For numerous reasons, self-monitoring data collection procedures should be incorporated into any anger control training program. From the clinician's perspective, they afford a more immediate, *in vivo* assessment of anger provocations, allow for an analysis of behavioral and situational patterns, provide low cost continuous data, and can be translated easily into role-play scripts generated by the adolescents themselves for use within the training groups.

Self–Monitoring Methodology

Depending upon the setting in which the training is being conducted, the skills and deficits of the target adolescents, and the types of information needed, different self-monitoring devices can be developed. These devices may vary according to structure (from highly structured checklists to informal diary-type entries), level of analysis (discrete physiological and cognitive responses to overall global evaluations of the anger experienced), timing of the data recording, and contingencies arranged for accurate completion.

Collection of self-monitoring data in a residential setting may be the easiest method because the routine structure of the adolescent's day and the numerous observers of behavior make it possible to predict problematic interactions and check on the accuracy of the adolescent's report. In our work we have found our Hassle Log (see Figure 2.1) the most appropriate in terms of the type and amount of information obtained and the adolescent's compliance rates. The Hassle Log is a single data sheet that requires a simple scanning and checking off of items by the target adolescent. Designed for use at a residential facility, it includes setting events and anger-provoking stimuli particular to this environment. The adolescent is instructed to complete one of these data sheets for every hassle he/she encounters. The adolescent must check situational factors, his/her own responses to the provocation, and then evaluate his/her performance and level of anger. There are always spaces for additional information should the adolescent feel like elaborating. Not only is the data sheet easy to read and complete, but it also provides the adolescent with the opportunity to indicate the other person's wrongdoings.

Usually these data sheets are provided in a notebook, so that the adolescent can easily fill out as many sheets as necessary. With lower-functioning clients, requesting a single data sheet between training sessions or structuring the initial part of the session to include an assisted hassle log completion is advisable. Further, some of the items are quantifiable, and the adolescent's behavior can be graphed over a period of time.

Obtaining Compliance with Self-Monitoring Procedures

Since the technique of self-monitoring requires that the adolescent record occurrences of his/her own behavior in the natural setting, compliance and cooperation with procedures are important. To understand how to ensure compliance, it is helpful to examine some reasons for noncompliance with self-monitoring assignments.

Understanding the Rationale. In order to complete the task at hand, the adolescent must not only understand the actual process of self-observation, evaluation of events and responses, and recording of actual data, but he/she must understand the reasons why these data are necessary. This rationale must be thoroughly

FIGURE 2.1. Hassle log self-monitoring device

```
                                    Date:_____
                                    Morn._____Aft._____Even._____

                              HASSLE LOG
                            Conflict Situations

Where were you?
          class_____        specialty class_____        off campus_____
        cottage_____              dining_____               other_____
            gym_____    outside/on campus_____       _____

What happened?
   Somebody teased me.                                                    _____
   Somebody took something of mine.                                       _____
   Somebody told me to do something.                                      _____
   Somebody was doing something I didn't like.                            _____
   Somebody started fighting with me.                                     _____
   I did something wrong.                                                 _____
   Other:_____
   _____          _____


Who was that somebody?
   another student_____  teacher_____  counselor_____
   parent_____  another adult_____  sibling_____

What did you do?
                hit back _____      told supervising adult _____
                ran away _____      walked away calmly _____
                  yelled _____             talked it out _____
                   cried _____                told peer _____
         broke something _____                 ignored _____
           was restrained _____     other _____
                                       _____

How did you handle yourself?
        1              2              3              4              5
      poorly       not so well       okay           good          great

How angry were you?
        1              2              3              4              5
   burning mad    really angry    moderately     mildly angry    not angry
                                     angry        but still OK     at all
```

explained prior to collecting any self-monitoring data. We have found that simple explanation and demonstration of self-monitoring behavior should be completed first. This should then be followed by a discussion of reasons for watching and recording one's own behavior. The clinician must make a case for needing immediate information about problem incidents, so that suggestions can be given in terms of handling them. Often, the adolescent will comply with self-monitoring in order to highlight how others are always provoking him. Further, the adolescent can be reminded that since the clinician is really very removed from the actual problem situations that the adolescent must face, self-monitoring information will assist the clinician in gaining a better understanding of just how tough things really are.

Understanding the Use of the Technology. The actual data sheets used for the process of recording and quantifying the data must be readable and understandable for the adolescent. Starting off with a demonstration and role play of the self-monitoring process will help to assess the adolescent's understanding of the technique. Sometimes a verbal quiz will help to prevent difficulties. The adolescent might be asked a series of "What if . . . how would you record this?" questions.

Competing Contingencies. If there are very strong reinforcers contingent upon not recording data or strong punishers contingent upon recording data, the adolescent will not comply with the self-monitoring procedure. Usually peers are the source of these consequences, and a careful analysis of each situation must be conducted prior to assigning self-monitoring. Further, if the adolescent has some unexpressed objectives (such as trying to get moved to another unit or getting his/her parents involved in therapy), then his/her noncompliance with the task may actually be quite functional. These contingencies must also be examined and altered, if necessary.

Reliability and Validity Issues

Clearly one of the major limitations of this low-cost, clinically relevant assessment method is the subjective nature of all data collected. Everyone asked to observe their own behavior and various setting events, and record this information following the occurrence of the event, will be influenced by their own perceptions of the events, memory for details, and the outcome of the anger provocation and the accompanying emotion. Adolescents will often record events in a way that implicates others in the initial provocation and then will plead their own case. But since the information they supply is not being used primarily for research purposes, these types of subjective biases actually *add* relevant clinical information. Misattributions of intent and blame and the distorted memory for sequences of aggressive behavior patterns, which are quite characteristic of adolescents with temper-control disorders, are best assessed and changed by self-monitoring technology. As the adolescent learns the cognitive-behavioral methods of anger control, his/her self-monitoring records will actually reflect changes in self-observation skills and cognitive appraisals of precipitating events.

The problem that occurs most frequently and that drastically reduces both the reliability of these data and the effectiveness of the treatment techniques is *non*recording of anger provocations. Often the adolescent will report that because there were no hassles during a given time period, there was no need to complete data sheets. This nonrecording may be a form of resistance or may be due to any of the factors cited above, and it must be addressed. Since the actual data sheets are often used for within-session role plays and the self-monitoring data are the only continuous evaluation measure with regard to treatment effectiveness, recording must be assured. It may be necessary to structure accuracy checks, which involves obtaining data from collaborating sources such as teachers, childcare staff, or parents. Asking them to keep a simple log of anger provocations in which the target adolescent was involved can serve as a reliability check with the adolescent's self-monitoring data. (Sometimes such a log simply serves as a reminder of quickly forgotten events.)

This teacher and/or parent cooperation may be done with or without the adolescent's knowledge, continuously or intermittently, and formally or informally. Certainly if this type of checking needs to be done with all of a group's members, a simplified checklist would be appropriate. Usually, however, group members will spontaneously provide very descriptive data about everyone else's behavior. In examining the validity of self-monitoring data collection procedures, several issues surface. Information obtained through self-monitoring is not likely to correlate well with other methods of assessment, due to the subjective distortions mentioned above. Further, this method may not even be measuring the behaviors of interest (overt and covert responses to anger provocations), but rather may only allow an assessment of the perceptual and cognitive abilities of the adolescent during stressful interactions. However, the richness of the data obtained and the therapeutic effectiveness of self-observation and recording are benefits that outweigh these psychometric inadequacies. Whatever the self-monitoring method measures is of interest to the therapist.

Paper–Pencil Measures

Introduction

One of the simplest methods of assessment for evaluating both individual and group behavior change as a result of anger control training is the use of paper-pencil type inventories. These devices can be easily administered to adolescents receiving treatment and to those who have frequent contact with the clients. When administered prior to the onset of treatment, following treatment, and at follow-up intervals, these data can provide quantification of changes made as a result of the treatment program. Some of these assessment instruments have normative data for comparison purposes.

Self-Report Inventories

These instruments, given to individual adolescents to complete prior to treatment, are easy to administer and score. They require that the adolescent read and understand each item and respond, usually on a Likert-type scale. Depending upon the population and the information desired, there are several devices that are recommended. Table 2.1 presents self-report instruments that are useful with adolescent populations.

Table 2.1. Adolescent Self-Report Instruments

Name of Inventory	Reference	General Item Content
Jesness Behavior Checklist	Jesness, 1966	14 subscales including anger control.
Children's Action Tendency Scale	Deluty, 1979	20-item forced choice inventory. 3 subscales; submissiveness, aggressiveness, and assertiveness.
Adolescent Assertion Expression Scale	Connor, Dann, & Twentyman, 1982	60-item inventory rated on Likert-type scale. 3 subscales; submissiveness, aggressiveness, and assertiveness.
Self-Control Rating Scale	Rosenbaum, 1980	36-item inventory designed to measure use of self-statements to control responding, application of problem-solving strategies, self-efficacy, and ability to delay gratification.
Personal Problem Inventory	Heppner, 1982	35-item inventory designed to assess perceptions of problem-solving behaviors and attitudes. Subscales are: problem solving confidence, approach-avoidance style, personal/self-control.
Anger Inventory	Novaco, 1975	90-item instrument that presents hypothetical anger-evoking situations. Responses made on a 5-point Likert scale indicating degree of anger.
Adolescent Problem Inventory	Freedman et al., 1978	44-item instrument designed to measure social competence in hypothetical problem situations.
Conflict Behavior Questionnaire	Prinz, Foster, Kent, & O'Leary, 1979	Measure of perceived communication conflict behavior at home. Completed by both adolescent and parent.
Rathus Assertion Inventory/Adolescent	Vaal, 1975	30-item or 19-item version of schedule designed to measure situational assertiveness.
Problem Inventory for Adolescent Girls	Gaffney & McFall, 1981	52-item inventory of hypothetical interpersonal conflict situations. Adolescents' role-played responses are scored on a 5-point scale indicating level of competence.
Means/ends Problem Solving Inventory	Shure & Spivack, 1972	Hypothetical problems that need alternate solutions; measures cognitive problem solving.
Children's Anger Inventory	Finch, Saylor, & Nelson, 1983	71-item inventory designed to measure children's probable anger responses to hypothetical situations. Completed via 4-point Likert pictorial scale.
Anger Control Inventory	Hoshmand & Austin, 1985	128-item inventory divided into two sections: situations that engender anger reactions and individual responses to anger-eliciting situations (15 subscales).
Matching Familiar Figures Test	Kagan, 1966	Match-to-sample measure of cognitive impulsivity on an impersonal task.
Porteus Mazes	Porteus, 1955	Perceptual motor measure of cognitive impulsivity.

Ratings by Others

There are also inventories that are completed by those persons having the most contact with the target adolescent. Usually completed by parents, teachers, or counselors, these inventories are easy to administer and allow for an assessment of the adolescent's increased anger control skills in the natural environment. Although the responses of those who have the most contact with the clients may be influenced by their relationship and operating environmental contingencies, these persons generally will provide an accurate appraisal of the adolescent's behavior. The inventory, selected on the basis of population and the target behaviors of interest, should be administered prior to the start of treatment and following treatment termination. Also, more than one person can provide these evaluations, but the same persons should do both the pre- and posttesting. Table 2.2 presents some of the checklists useful with adolescent populations.

Table 2.2. Adolescent Checklist Instruments

Name of Inventory	Reference	General Item Content
Jesness Behavior Checklist	Jesness, 1966	110-item inventory, 14 subscales including anger and social control.
Adolescent Antisocial Behavior Checklist	Ostrov, Marohn, Offer, Curtiss, & Feczko, 1980	Behavioral scales consisting of 35 items sampling delinquent behaviors. Subscales include: violence toward self, others, property, and nonviolent antisocial behavior.
Self-Control Rating Scale for Children	Kendall & Wilcox, 1979	Scale, designed for elementary children, contains 33 items indicating cognitive and behavioral skills related to self-control. Can be used by both teachers and parents.
Child Behavior Profile	Achenbach & Edelbrock, 1979	118-item checklist of problem behaviors completed by parent. Subscales include: somatic complaints, withdrawal, hyperactive, aggressive, delinquent. Use with adolescents up to age 16.
Assess	Prinz, Swan, Liebert, Weintraub, & Neale, 1978	45-item peer sociometric measure with 5 subscales including aggression/disruptiveness.
Behavior Problem Checklist	Quay, 1977	58-item checklist indicating a 3-point scale for rating problem behaviors. Subscales include: Conduct problems, personality problems, inadequacy-immaturity, and socialized-delinquency.
Adolescent Symptom Checklist	Kohn, Koretsky, & Haft (1979)	33-item checklist containing two subscales: Apathy-withdrawal and anger-defiance.

In addition, rating scales or checklists concerning anger outbursts and/or aggressive behaviors have been developed on a case by case basis. Although not psychometrically developed, these types of scales are useful because they are tailored to particular target populations and reflect training techniques and skills specific to the intervention program. Kolko et al. (1981) devised a 14-item Ward Adjustment and an 18-item Therapy Adjustment Scale to measure the staff's and the therapists' perceptions of adolescents' social skills in naturalistic settings. Following a combined anger control/social skills training program, adolescents were rated as approaching maximal levels of adjustment.

Role-Play Assessments

Introduction

Direct behavioral observations or parent/staff recordings of adolescent aggressive behavior may not be a feasible way to collect data, given the time and cost constraints. Although the more direct the assessment tool, the more reliable and valid the information obtained, clinical objectives may not require such rigorous standards. An alternate method that is both flexible and comprehensive in regard to the type of data available is role-play or analogue assessment (Beck, Forehand, Neeper, & Baskin, 1982). Observations of the adolescent's behavior are conducted during staged conflict situations. This allows the clinician to control the setting events and elicit the behaviors of interest, code and quantify the information in any number of ways, and tap the range of the adolescent's skill repertoire. This assessment method is not only practical and portable, but it has a therapeutic value as well. Adolescents who engage in structured role plays may learn alternate behaviors from the model who is interacting with them, or they may try new responses. The consequences that follow the target adolescent's responses may influence their occurrence and thus alter the adolescent's repertoire. Further, role-play assessments provide an arena for spontaneous occurrences and allow for an appraisal of eliciting stimuli. Some caution is recommended, however, in generalizing data obtained from this structured analogue assessment strategy (cf. Bellack, Hersen, & Lamparski, 1979).

Role Play Assessment Methodology

Scripts. In order to begin to conduct role-play assessments, a semistructured script is needed. This merely consists of a scene (or stimulus setting), a lead-in narration, and a confederate or co-actor who provides the provocation prompts. In keeping with the goals of the anger-control training program, the scenes that are most relevant are those involving interpersonal conflict situations. These scenarios can be replications of observed or recorded conflicts that have happened to the adolescent or to other adolescents, events that have been recorded via the self-monitoring methodology, or standardized situations used in a training program. However the scenes are chosen, they must be appropriate to the particular population with which the clinician is working. In general, we have found that the majority of conflicts center around the following themes: conflict with authority figures, loss of property or privileges, teasing or threatening from peers, being falsely blamed or accused, and peer competition. (See Table 2.3 for examples of a conflict role play.)

The narrator should set up the conflict scene with a brief introduction, and the co-actor should begin with a scripted lead-in line. Following that, the remainder of the role play depends upon the structure imposed. We have found it helpful to continue the assessment through five or six exchanges before terminating and to allow the co-actor to continue with provocation statements. Finally, the use of props to further simulate real-life situations is helpful as well.

Instructions

Adolescents who will be participating in role-play assessments will need both a rationale for the activity and general instructions to guide them. We have presented these assessments as a "before–after" type of test to see how well the adolescent handles him/herself in difficult situations. Role playing should be defined to the adolescent as "acting as you might act if this ever happened to you or as you have acted in the past." Usually adolescents will then inquire as to whether or not they can use their "everyday language." They should be encouraged to be as natural as possible, but it should be explained that they must stop the scene when

Table 2.3. Examples of Conflict Role-Play Scripts

Script 1:	Interpersonal Conflict Situation
Narrator:	You are watching your favorite TV show. What is your favorite show? Okay you're watching __. John comes in and after a minute turns the channel.
John	I don't like this program, it's for babies.
You respond:	
Script 2:	Interpersonal Conflict Situation
Narrator:	There is Eddie playing with a basketball that is yours. You go over and ask to have the ball because you want to play with another friend. Eddie gets mad.
Eddie:	I'm not done with the ball. I'm still playing, man. Just wait a half second and I'll give it to you.
You respond:	
Script 3:	Interpersonal Conflict Situation
Narrator:	You dropped a dollar a minute ago on the couch, and you just realized it. You go back to get the dollar, and there is Ted with a dollar in his hand on the couch. You tell him you dropped the dollar and would like it back.
Ted:	It's mine. I found it and I'm not giving it back. Now get outta here!
You respond:	

instructed to do so. A final word should be said about physical boundaries; adolescents are not to use physical force. Some adolescents may seem shy or reluctant to participate in the role plays, but with some cajoling or with the trainer modeling the role play first to desensitize the adolescent to the anxiety-provoking elements, most will then comply.

Behavioral Coding

When using role plays for assessment purposes, it is necessary to decide which of the adolescent's responses to code for data collection. Since the anger control program is designed to increase self-control skills and reduce aggressive responding, the coding system should include these behaviors. Behavioral categories must be clearly defined so that data recorders can reliably code the role plays. We have used standardized data coding sheets modeled on the definitions provided by Frederiksen et al. (1976) for the assessments of groups that we have run. However, when working with individual adolescents, this coding may be individualized. (See Figure 2.2 for an example of a role-play assessment coding sheet.) Kolko et al. (1981) provide useful scoring criteria for specific social skills (response latency, eye contact, facial expression, voice loudness, and content of verbal response) that relate to making an effective response to provocation.

FIGURE 2.2. Role-play assessment coding sheet

Subject: _____   Rater: _____
Testing: _____
Date: _____

Irrelevant Comments	Hostile Comments	Inappropriate Requests	Appropriate Requests

In Pocket	Gesture	At Side	Positive Physical	Negative Physical

Duration of Scene: _____
Duration of eye contact: _____
Duration subject speech: _____
Ratio: _____

Loudness

1	2	3	4	5
too soft/ whisper		just right		too loud/ yelling

Overall global rating

1	2	3	4	5	6	7
very passive			very assertive			very aggressive

In general, both verbal and nonverbal aggressive responses should be recorded, as well as appropriate responses to the co-actor, voice loudness, use of discrete anger control techniques, and outcome. Counting the frequency for each behavioral category, per scene, provides an easily quantifiable measure. If at all possible, videotaping the role-played conflict situations is highly recommended. This will provide a permanent product and thus make the actual coding of data easier. Further, the adolescent will greatly benefit from evaluating his/her own behavior and this will aid in teaching self-observation skills. We have also used these videotapes as aids in teaching self-monitoring and self-evaluation skills. An added bonus that emerges with the inclusion of videotape equipment is that the opportunity to be on camera/TV can often serve as a within-group reinforcer for appropriate behavior. Finally, this permanent product can be useful when providing feedback to parents and other persons involved with the adolescent. Table 2.4 provides an example of a role-played provocation scenario.

This brief interaction would then be scored to attempt to quantify the aggressive verbalizations and the accompanying nonverbals that the target adolescent emitted. Simply by coding the verbal responses, the data sheet might look something like this:

1. foul language   3
2. hostile comments   3
3. inappropriate requests   1
4. appropriate requests   0
5. appropriate comments   1
6. assertion/anger control techniques   2
7. irrelevant comments   2

Several scenes could be presented and data summed up from all scenes. We recommend generating a pool of sample situations relevant to the particular setting and population with which you work using a standard set for each group member if you are running a group, or for each adolescent in individual treatment. This allows for comparisons across individuals and collection of normative data for your population. Further, it facilitates more wide-scale program evaluations.

Pre- and Posttesting

Pretest data obtained from coding analogue role plays can be used for a variety of purposes. First, it provides a good initial screen for gross skill deficits (lower functioning clients may not have the verbal skills required to participate in a structured role play and may not benefit from this cognitive-behavioral training program) and a set of data upon which to form more homogeneous groups. Clearly, not all aggressive adolescents are lacking in anger control skills, but rather they do not use them in certain stimulus situations. These adolescents may perform won-

Table 2.4. Examples of Role-Play Interactions

Narrator:	You're watching your favorite TV show on your unit. All of a sudden, another resident barges into the room and changes the channel. He tells you to get out of *his* chair.
Resident:	Hey, get out of *my* chair. Better yet, get out of here. We ain't watching that baby show anymore. Go find a baby to play with.
Target Adolescent:	I was here first, plus, I asked yesterday if I could watch this. I earned all of my points for school.
Resident:	I don't give two sh__ts about your points. I told you where to go.
Target:	F__ck off. I ain't moving. Get out of my face.
Resident:	Yes you are, you as__hole. Or else I'll be moving you myself, you fat slob. So beat it and keep your hands off the TV.
Target:	I don't have to take this crap from you, airbrain. You ain't even got no place to visit on weekends. Yeh, you're real tough; so tough that nobody gives a sh__t about you. I could take you down in a minute. You as__hole. Why don't you go drink some nails.
Narrator:	Okay. Time!

derfully on role-play tests, but never exhibit these skills in their natural environments. This would then require a close examination of both the contingencies controlling the performance of said self-management and the possible interfering anxiety that would lead to a performance deficit. Indeed, we have found that many adolescents perform perfectly on role plays, indicating not only that they have the skills, but that they also are aware of the expectations and demands of the situation. Other adolescents do not exhibit this level of social maturity and require more basic skills training. It may be helpful to group these adolescents as homogeneously as possible.

When conducting posttraining role-play assessments, it is preferable to use a new set of scenarios so as to minimize the effects of testing. These new scenes also provide a measure of generalization of anger control skills to situations not previously practiced. If the adolescents have learned how to control their anger, the data from posttesting should reveal fewer instances of aggressive verbalizations and more frequent use of assertive statements and other arousal reduction techniques (pausing, taking a deep breath, ignoring the other's escalating responses). This will not only provide data for evaluation of individual changes, but will also validate the effectiveness of the training program.

Planned and Unplanned In Vivo Barbs

The high demands of the testing situation and the "safety" provided by the rules of the role play may greatly influence the adolescent's performance. Thus, the clinician may not get a true picture of natural responding. To help obtain more natural data, we have developed a "barb" technique that is used both as an assessment and as a treatment. Based on the original technique developed by Kaufmann and

Wagner in 1972, the "barb" is a provocation statement made directly to the target adolescent in situations other than the actual training one. Kolko et al. (1981) employed a similar technique of ward simulations to analyze social skills of target adolescents in the natural environment. In our programs, these barbs are usually delivered by staff members, teachers, or parents, depending on the adolescent. This results in a controlled but more natural conflict situation between the adolescent and an authority figure.

During the first phases of the training program, the adolescent is issued a warning first, "I'm going to barb you," and then the barb is delivered. (Example: "What are you doing in the TV room when I told you that you were on restriction?") The person delivering the barb is required to note and record the adolescent's responses. This could be either a verbatim report or a simple checklist format. Early barbs should be inaccurate in content to facilitate the adolescent's discrimination that a barb signals anger control skills. Then gradually the content of the barbs should more closely approximate realistic inquiries made by staff members. The barbs should be provided by a variety of persons, in a variety of stimulus situations, and on an intermittent schedule in order to ensure generalization to all. Clearly, the use of this technique as an assessment tool is questionable because of its highly interactive nature. In fact, although data are recorded and used for assessment, the barb may be better labeled a transfer strategy or an independent variable check. This is especially true when using unplanned barbs. During the later phases of training and during subsequent follow-up periods, barbs are given without warning, but the same recording procedure is used. Since no signal is provided, the adolescent's responses are presumed to be natural. (See Table 2.5 for examples of barbs provided by parents and by inpatient staff.)

In summary, the use of this analogue assessment method enables the clinician to structure a situation to obtain a direct observation of the behaviors of interest. Although the adolescent's responses are influenced by the demand characteristics of the assessment setting, data obtained from coding pre- and posttraining performances can help to evaluate discrete individual behavior change. The extension of this assessment method to the barb format allows an estimate of generalization of behavior change across stimulus situations and maintenance across time. Further,

Table 2.5. Examples of Barbs Provided by Parents, Teachers, or Staff

- "I thought I told you to keep your hand out of my pocketbook! Now return the $20 you took."

- "Hey, I know you were involved in that fight on the unit — you'll have to pay for the broken furniture."

- "I got a call today from the school — apparently you haven't been to school all week. Now you'll be grounded for two months."

- "That shirt doesn't belong to you. Take it off and give it back."

- "Don't give me dirty looks. I can place you on restriction."

- "I know I promised to play some ball with you, but I really don't feel like you deserve it."

the use of role-play assessments builds the foundation for the numerous behavior rehearsals of newly acquired skills during the anger control training program. Finally, the cognitive problem-solving skills that are crucial to the development of anger control can be most readily assessed through the spontaneous generation of alternate solutions to hypothetical problems. Clearly, the role-play assessment strategy provides invaluable information and serves a therapeutic function.

Direct Observation Assessment Strategies

Introduction

Those familiar with behavioral assessment goals and methods know that the most objective and comprehensive strategy is direct observation. The process of defining target behaviors, observing and recording their occurrences in the natural environment, and analyzing these data provides the most direct assessment. Additionally, these data can be collected continuously, thereby providing an extremely sensitive index to measure changes in the adolescent's responding. Although this method requires much preplanning and considerable time on the part of observers and data analyzers, we recommend obtaining these data if at all possible. It must be mentioned, however, that the very nature of the responses that accompany anger provocation makes this a difficult task. Usually, the accompanying aggressive behavior, whether verbal or nonverbal, is emitted rather discretely. If the adolescent is aware that direct observations of his/her behavior are being conducted, he/she will exert some control over responses that would otherwise be rather severe in both frequency and intensity. Aggressive responses, when observed directly, would be performed in a less obvious fashion. Also, the cognitive and physiological responses that are modification targets in the anger control training program are not readily assessed by this method, since they cannot be observed. But approximations of aggressive behavior and appropriate social skills required for resolution of interpersonal conflict situations can be observed.

Direct Observation Methodology

An operational definition of each target behavior of interest is needed before starting. These definitions must be very clear and must delineate all the parameters of the responses, including a verbal description of the responses to be observed and requirements for inclusion and exclusion. A listing of examples of actual target responses is helpful. (See Table 2.6 for examples of operational definitions for aggressive behaviors.)

Measurement Devices

The method measurement of overt aggressive responses can be either a frequency, duration, or interval recording. If the behaviors that have been operationally defined have an easily observable onset and offset and the length of the

Table 2.6. Operational Definitions for Aggressive Behaviors

Tease:	Provocative statements directed toward another student or adult. Include ridiculing, name calling, taunting, picking on, and other nagging or provoking verbal responses. Exclude friendly, playful teasing and other statements which are accompanied by smiles and laughter by both students. Do *not* include threats to harm another person or another's property. Examples: 1. = "Hah, hah, you got in trouble." (mild) 2. = "Man, you are really a cry baby." (moderate) 3. = "You ugly S.O.B." (severe)
Argue:	A three-statement sequence of negative verbal provocations. Mark this category if you observe or hear a verbal fight or screaming match involving two or more students including the target student. Include any verbal provocations which occur in sequence, such as teases, ownership statements, refusals, denials, and other verbal responses with negative effect and meaning. Exclude threats, playful arguing, and true debates. Examples: 1. = "Get lost." "No, I won't." "Just leave me alone." (mild) 2. = "You jerk." "Don't call *me* names." "I'll do what I want." (moderate) 3. = "Give it back." "It's mine, so lay off." "You liar. You stole it out of my room." (Severe)
Threat:	A verbal statement or physical gesture to hurt another person or destroy something belonging to another. Verbal statements must include a behavioral referrent to aggressive responding, such as "I'm gonna break your arm." Gestures may include fist swinging, a raised belt or stick, etc. If physical contact is made to other person or property, mark both *Threat* and *Hit* or *Damage* categories. Exclude playful, good-natured threats ("I'll get the boogie man after you!") and threats that are unrealistic in terms of the behavioral repertoire of student ("I'll crush your mother with my foot."). Include any threat which the student may be able to carry out. Examples: 1. = "I'm gonna let the air out of your tires." (mild) 2. = "I'll smack your face if you do that." (moderate) 3. = "I'm gonna break every bone in your body." "I'm gonna kill you." (severe)
Hit:	Aggressive behaviors toward another person which may produce pain or injury. Physical contact must be made with a part of target student's body or an object with which he/she has contact. Mark only if you actually observe the aggressive act. Include shoving, hitting, slapping, punching, kicking, pinching, throwing objects, etc. Exclude playful or friendly contact performed in a positive context (smiles and laughter). Examples: 1. = A swift kick in the butt. (mild) 2. = Several punches in the arm. (moderate) 3. = Blow to the head. (severe)

response is not of interest, frequency recording is recommended. This entails simply defining the time period of observation (for example, a 30-minute block during a morning class) and keeping a tally of each time the behaviors of interest occur. Summing up this tally at the end of the observation session and at the end of the day, week, or month will provide the data points that can be graphed and evaluated.

If the duration of the behaviors of interest is the modification target (such as length of physical tantrums or length of screaming matches), then duration recording would be appropriate. This entails noting the time of onset and offset of the behavior of interest and summing up the total duration during specified time periods.

The recording method that may be most comprehensive, especially if observing several adolescents from an anger control group or coding several categories of aggressive responding, is interval recording. Again, an observation period must be defined (such as a half hour), but an observation interval must also be defined. This is usually a 1-minute interval in which each behavior of interest is recorded as either occurring or not occurring. If a behavior occurs more than once during an interval, it is only recorded as having occurred once. The observer can easily scan the target adolescents during the interval and note occurrence or nonoccurrence. These data are then summarized in terms of the percent of intervals in which the target responses occurred per observation session.

This type of recording method was used during pilot work in a single-subject evaluation of the anger control training program (Feindler, 1979). The data were collected each day during three separate 30-minute observation sessions for the duration of the 12-week study. The actual data recording sheet is presented in Figure 2.3. Observations were conducted in both the classroom (from behind a one-way observation mirror) and in a cottage setting at a residential facility for juveniles. Data provided continuous feedback for staff and therapists and were visually displayed for a general evaluation of the adolescent's progress.

Clearly, a direct observation assessment is neither practical nor necessary in all anger control interventions. When developing a new treatment package, however, it is desirable to collect such types of data so that both problems and positive behavior change can be noted immediately. If at all possible, data probes should be

Date: _____   Rater: _____
Target Student: _____   Class or Cottage No.: _____
Time Block: from _____ to _____

Please use the following severity ratings when marking behavior categories:
             1 = mild   2 = moderate   3 = severe

Behavior	1	2	3	4	5	6	7	8	9	10	Comments
Tease											
Argue											
Threat											
Hit											
In Fight											
Start Fight											
Damage											

FIGURE 2.3. Direct observation recording sheet

completed. This would entail observation and recording of clearly defined behaviors in the natural setting on an intermittent basis. Although a good deal of information is lost, this is more desirable than not collecting any direct observation data. The data sheet, the method of recording, and the observation schedule can be simplified enough to permit the collection of some direct observation data.

Once the observers have been selected, a training segment must be included. First, the observers need to have a clear rationale for collecting the data. It is also important to observe behavior as it occurs in the natural environment so as to measure the client's behavior change. Next, a careful description of each of the target behaviors, the recording device, and the process of recording must be given. Observers can be briefed on the details of the operational definitions and how to record occurrences of each target behavior. Behavior rehearsals in which the observers practice making the recordings with the coaching of a staff member can be very useful. If at all possible, have the observers work in independent pairs when conducting the observations (parents across the room from each other, teachers' aides in different part of the classroom, etc.). This will allow a check on the accuracy of the data recording through a comparison of data from each observer. This is called a *reliability check*. Although there are numerous requirements for conducting reliability checks and several methods of calculating the actual agreement scores for pairs of observers, this may not be feasible in the clinical setting. A simple method would be to compare the two data sheets by a simple percent agreement, accepting anything above the 80% mark.

If direct observation sessions are not to be conducted on a continuous basis, the schedule of the intermittent observation sessions must be carefully planned. It is necessary to conduct several observations prior to the implementation of the anger control training program. This provides baseline data against which behavior during and subsequent to treatment can be compared. Direct observation probes should be conducted several times during the course of treatment, preferably as often as possible, and during the follow-up phase. Analyses of the various data stages will allow for an evaluation of components of the treatment program and direct observation of possible antecedent consequent events occurring in the natural environment that may be interfering with treatment.

Selection of observation times should also be made to maximize the probability of observing the behaviors of interest, namely aggressive and acting-out behaviors. Anger provocations may occur more reliably in some situations, and these should be targeted for observation. The clinician must make sure that the observers know the observation schedule and that they keep to it.

A note of caution: Do not be tempted to use already existing forms of data collection in your facility. Too often these data do not represent actual occurrences of the adolescent's aggressive behavior, but rather the staff's consequation behavior (i.e., fines for disruptive behavior).

Other Sources of Dependent Variables

Institutional Data

There are numerous sources of archival and continuous data available in any institutional setting. These data are routinely collected as part of already existing programs or as institutional requirements, and they may easily be incorporated into an evaluation of an anger control training program. For example, data collected to evaluate stress inoculation training of an aggressive hospitalized female included frequency of "write ups" in her chart for aggression, frequency of seclusions, and frequency of "write ups" for prosocial behavior (Bristline & Frieden, 1984). These easily obtainable sources may be the sole evaluation data in a setting where staff members are already overloaded with paperwork or seem resistant to collecting additional data. Many staff who work with aggressive adolescents are usually quite leery of some new program designed to alter the adolescent's behavior. These data may include:

School Records
- absences
- detentions
- suspensions
- demerits
- expulsions
- rule violations
- class cuts
- academic data
- grades in classes
- standardized testing
- homework completion
- error rates
- test grades
- teacher evaluations
- yearly reports

Inpatient/Ward Data
- daily nurse's notes
- emergency team calls
- restrictions
- confinements
- need for restraints or medication
- fines or other response-cost measures
- rule violations
- altercations with others (in most inpatient settings, these sorts of infractions must be documented with much detail and may serve as useful sources of data)

- elopements
- transfers to other settings
- other program data
- loss of privileges
- program achievements
- placements in less restrictive environments
- psychological evaluations and testings that may indicate improvements in interpersonal functioning or socio-emotional development
- recidivism rates
- adjustment to alternate placements following termination of anger control training
- home visits or other off-campus activities
- frequency and success monitored in terms of behavior while away from inpatient setting

Outpatient Settings
- setting and keeping appointments
- being on time
- behavior during sessions (how cooperative is adolescent during sessions with respect to verbal participation, eye contact, volunteering of relevant information, etc.)
- homework completion (comprehensiveness, accuracy, etc. These types of data are the subjective evaluations of the therapist and can be completed by a weekly postsession checklist.)
- weekly behavior checklists completed by family members or by significant others (These data should target the observed anger control methods used and noticeable differences in the adolescent's ability to control his temper.)

Community Data. There are numerous sources available from community agencies already collecting data that can be used to further evaluate the effectiveness of your anger control intervention. These sources of data include school records (such as truancy and/or attendance rates, school violations), court and police contacts (with particular reference to the types of infractions and whether or not they were related to the target behavior problems), reports from probation officers or other court-appointed personnel, evaluations from the actual court contacts, and the dispositions of the cases. If the adolescent is involved in any other community organization such as sports clubs, scout groups, rap groups, and the like, you may also obtain reports of attendance and any potential anger incidents (i.e., were there fights in which the target adolescent was involved?).

All of the above activities are staffed by both professional and paraprofessional staff who could provide more subjective evaluations of the adolescent's abilities to control him/herself during activities and direct anger provocations. These evaluation data can be collected via simple Likert-type rating scales that represent low response costs for the respondent and can be compared over time. A note of caution in terms of how the actual data collection is implemented: When working with adolescents, the trust relationship is of utmost importance. This means that any inquiries, whether formal or informal, that you wish to make concerning the adolescent's behavior must by some means be made known to the adolescent. With routine record collection, there may be less of an issue concerning your access to information, but any new data that might be requested (such as subjective rating scales completed by the probation counselor) should be cleared with the adolescent. If this is done in the positive guise of "checking out how well you are doing," or "troubleshooting before the problem really gets out of hand," it will further the adolescent's understanding of why this is important.

Assessment Issues When Using Institutional Data

The term *institutional data* is used to delineate those data that are archival in nature or easily obtainable by slightly altering the already existing institutional data collection systems. Given the indirect approach to this type of data collection and analysis, there are several issues that need to be considered.

Unreliability of Sources. In order to evaluate accurately changes in the adolescent's behavior and thereby the effectiveness of the anger control intervention program, the clinician must be able to trust the data sources. Because of this, those personnel who are providing data may be subject to contingencies controlling their behavior. For example, take the case of a youth who was already in a program for multisuspended youth in an inner city junior high school (Feindler et al., 1984). This 14-year-old's behavior was often poorly controlled, and he evidenced frequent verbal aggression toward his main teacher. Although the teacher knew he was involved in a specialized anger control program in which his behavior was markedly improved (and this was substantiated by reports from other teachers and our own direct observation during role-played provocations), she continued to maintain that he required teaching in a more restrictive environment. Clearly, if she was to be successful at engineering a transfer from this within-school program to either another special education class or a residential setting, she needed to continue to evaluate his behavior as unacceptable and beyond control. This teacher consistently gave the target student the lowest evaluation on both paper and pencil measures as well as more subjective evaluations.

Given the numerous tasks that many paraprofessionals and professionals must complete in the normal course of their duties, the response-cost contingencies for completing even a single additional sheet may be overwhelming. Sometimes, however, in light of the goals of the helping professions, these respondents will willingly fill out the questionnaire but will not pay close attention to their answers. Finally, the clinician must be careful not to make the data collection system too complex. This definitely reduces both compliance and accuracy. The simpler the data sheet, the lower the response cost for completing it. Likewise, the more meaningful the task is to the respondent, the more likely the clinician is to get usable information.

Inference and Indirect Sources of Data. Above all, when using institutional data sources, the clinician must remember that these data do not reflect the adolescent's behaviors directly. Furthermore, there are significant time delays and interpretations that accompany these data. Whenever the behavioral assessor is unable to obtain direct observation data, he/she must settle for some level of inference. The level of inference is highest when using data that reflect staff behavior rather than adolescent behavior. For example, if fine and/or token earnings with respect to aggressive behavior on the ward or in the classroom are being used, these data do not reflect the adolescent's aggressive responses. We assume that the adolescent's behavior elicits a chain of staff member behavior that includes observing the aggressive response, evaluating the type and severity of the response, matching the appropriate consequence to the response, and then delivering said consequence in the appropriate fashion. Needless to say, there is room for much variation in this chain of events, and the resultant token or fine is more the result of staff behavior. This sequence can be applied to all settings in which institutional data are collected.

Difficulties in Quantifying These Data. Due to the many varied sources of data already collected in the institutional setting, the task of quantifying them in order to facilitate data analysis becomes a rather challenging one. Clearly, some sources are more discrete than others (number of police contacts, school attendance rates, grades, fines received for physical aggression, etc.). The narrative descriptions of actual anger provocations that run rampant through nurses' notes on inpatient units and the like actually provide rich sources of data concerning anger control abilities. These data may not only be almost illegible at times, but may also be incomplete and highly subjective, and caution is urged when using these data. However, rating scales by which an outside evaluator could examine these data are feasible. (Figure 2.4 presents a possible coding sheet.) It may be possible to develop a coding system that would help to quantify the intensity/severity and the topography of the anger incident.

FIGURE 2.4. Coding sheet for institutional records

Date: _____	Cottage No.: _____	
Shift: _____		
Incident	Frequency	Kids
AWOL	_____	_____
Emergency Response Team called	_____	_____
Aggression toward child	_____	_____
Aggression toward adult	_____	_____
Property damage	_____	_____
Stealing	_____	_____
Physical restraint used	_____	_____
Seclusion	_____	_____
Medication required	_____	_____

ASSESSMENT FOR
CLINICAL RESEARCH AND
PROGRAM EVALUATION

Introduction

Assessment strategies for research and program evaluation purposes must meet the requirements of experimental rigor and be readily incorporated into the chosen research designs. The use of reliable and valid assessment tools is of paramount importance in the description and manipulation of variables that may affect behavior change. Certainly, the anger control training package contains a host of techniques that make cause-and-effect relationships difficult to establish when one takes into account variables such as population, treatment setting, characteristics of the trainers, and other contingencies controlling the adolescent's behavior.

In order to answer scientific questions concerning the functional relationships between independent variables (such as cognitive-behavioral, self-management techniques) and dependent variables (such as performance on assessment tasks or behavior in the natural environment), the collection of data and the implementation of treatment must be done in a fairly structured manner. There are many empirical questions concerning the efficacy of the various components of this package that still require investigation, and it is hoped that clinicians using the program will collect data to these ends.

Single Subject Evaluations

Anyone who has worked with adolescents knows that there is a high degree of variability in each of them and between them. Sometimes they fail to improve, sometimes they improve rather spontaneously, and sometimes they show cyclical variability (Hersen & Barlow, 1976). In order to search out the sources of this variability, it is helpful to employ a single subject research design in which behavior is measured repeatedly, while various aspects of the independent variable are manipulated. In simpler terms, this would involve the measurement of an adolescent's behavior in a continuous fashion, such as via direct observation of aggressive behavior in the classroom or assessment of repeated analogue-type probes. Following a baseline period, single components of the anger control training package would be introduced, and behavior change would be analyzed.

In order to determine whether it was solely the treatment strategy that effected change, other experimental phases would need to be added. A reversal design in which the independent variable is then withdrawn and observations are made during a return to baseline phase would *not* be appropriate in this case, since learning has (hopefully) occurred. A multiple baseline design across individuals in the same environment would be more appropriate. Treatment is applied in sequence to each subject, with the baseline for each subject increasing in length. The clinical researchers can be assured that the treatment variable is effective if a change appears in the target behaviors after said variable has been applied and the rate of behavior for the untreated subjects remains relatively constant.

There are other potentially useful single subject designs, and the reader is referred to Hersen and Barlow (1976) or Bellack and Hersen (1984) for information and discussion of repeated measurement techniques, statistical analyses, and replication procedures.

Group Evaluations

If anger control training is being conducted in a group format, a group research design may be more feasible. In the simplest form, this type of design requires two groups (a treatment and a control group), random assignment of subjects to groups, and reliable and valid measures administered in a pre and posttreatment fashion. In order to analyze data with any degree of power, a group size of at least eight subjects is recommended. The control group may consist of adolescents who are not receiving cognitive-behavioral treatment for anger control, but who may be receiving other types of therapy for their anger control problems.

Ideally, the control group subjects and the treatment group subjects should be matched for age, sex, diagnostic category, behavior problems, and treatment history. This, and the necessary random assignment, is usually impossible to accomplish in the applied settings in which these adolescents are found. Facility administrators will rarely allow the clinical researcher to control all of these variables. In one study addressing some of these concerns, we (Feindler et al., 1986) chose two already established wards of adolescents and then randomly selected which ward was to receive treatment first. Also, our pretest data on both units was analyzed and revealed no significant differences, thus supporting the initial equivalence of the groups.

The data from group designs can be analyzed using a host of statistical procedures. If continuous group data is available (such as repeated measurements of the group members' behavior in the group or in other natural settings), these should be graphed across time. Although these are not direct observation data, but rather response-cost contingencies placed on aggressive behavior, the graphic display of continuous data for both the treatment and the control groups helps to analyze changes related to treatment implementation.

Again, the reader is referred to either Bellack and Hersen (1984) or Hersen and Barlow (1976) for a discussion of alternate research design strategies, such as quasiexperimental designs, in which concerns related to applied settings are addressed.

GENERAL ASSESSMENT ISSUES

When employing any of the assessment strategies outlined in this chapter, there are several issues to consider. First is the issue of willingness to volunteer. Adolescents who have consented to the anger control training program must also consent to the various assessment procedures that will be used. Without sensitizing the adolescent in such a way as to alter his/her natural behavior during observations, role plays and the like, he/she must be given a rationale for the repeated assessments and asked to volunteer. In our work, we have found that the rationale that is most understandable to adolescents is that of program evaluation. Simply stated, data must be collected before and after the program to see if any changes were made and if the program is worth repeating. One should stay away from any direct notion of psychological testing, because the majority of acting-out adolescents have already been down this road and will not willingly participate.

To further ensure voluntary and cooperative participation in the assessment process, several guarantees can be made to adolescents. Confidentiality of the results from the assessment devices should be assured. If the clinician is going to use the data for any sort of research purposes, a more comprehensive, signed consent form that assures anonymity of the data must be obtained as well. Further, adolescents should be assured that there will be no contingencies placed upon the results of the various assessments. Hopefully this will encourage them to respond naturally. Lastly, the clinician should allow adolescents to view their videotapes or see the actual data that were collected following the termination of the treatment/research program.

These same issues may arise when asking others to participate in the assessment of adolescents. Staff members need a similar rationale for the assessment phase, and since their cooperation is usually critical, careful thought should be given to this. Certainly the response cost of data collection procedures should be minimized, and help should be available (such as time to complete inventories and trouble shooting with observation instruments). In general, staff are usually willing to cooperate as long as they understand the reasons for the assessments and there are no competing contingencies operating on them.

Comprehensive assessment prior to beginning any treatment program is essential. Without some kind of data collection on target behavior problems before, during, and after treatment, there will be no reliable way to evaluate the efficacy of the intervention. And although most clinical settings do not permit the extensive data collection that we advocate, some type of pre- and posttesting evaluation of already existing dependent measures and self-monitoring during the actual anger control training program is critical. A multimodal approach to assessment, which includes several different sources of data for evaluation (Kolko et al., 1981), is the most desirable and accurate way to assess a program's effectiveness.

Chapter 3

Implementing Group Anger Control Treatment for Agencies and Institutions

CONDUCTING GROUP ANGER CONTROL TRAINING

It has been approximately 5 years since the cognitive-behaviorally oriented group (and individual) adolescent anger control program, The Art of Self-Control, was developed. During this time, over 500 group sessions have been provided to 443 adolescents who had experienced problems controlling their aggressive or explosive behaviors in previous academic, home, or residential environments.

Training and Experience of Group Leaders

Any professional who has the dedicated commitment, enthusiasm, and motivation to work with groups of aggressive adolescents has the potential to become an effective leader of a cognitive-behaviorally oriented adolescent anger control program. While the ultimate responsibility for change rests upon the members, the group leader must possess the leadership skills necessary to create an atmosphere that is conducive to constructive learning and individual change. We concur with Merritt and Walley (1977) who describe the ideal group leader as "creative, non-judgmental, democratic, excited, exciting, sharing, inspiring, strong, sensitive, perceptive, a member of the team, patient, growing, learning, open, alive, honest, exploring, feeling, you!" (p. 13).

Group Leader Responsibilities

The main responsibility of the group leader is to facilitate the therapeutic process for each group member. With this in mind, the leader brings particular individuals together into a group and makes overall policy decisions concerning meeting time and place, frequency of sessions, and the general manner in which he/she plans to conduct the group. Once sessions begin, the leader continues to make decisions concerning, for example, which aspects of the sessions require particular attention, when and how to intervene, and so on. In addition to having exceptional knowledge of the subject material he/she plans to offer, the leader must be flexible in terms of modifying planned session objectives, subject material (e.g., homework) and/or therapeutic techniques in order to facilitate and maintain members' interest, motivation, and continued progress toward short- and long-term goals. As facilitator, the leader must be exceptionally skillful in observing each member's behavioral cues at any time (e.g., just before, during, or immediately after each session) and assessing the various emotional and attitudinal states that operate within the group. This unique perspective enables the leader to empathize with the members' affective experience and comment objectively on the emotions expressed.

Group Counseling Skills

In a similar vein, the group leader must be skillful in clarifying, summarizing, and interpreting group members' verbal comments without altering their basic meaning. The effective leader must be able to maintain the group's focus on relevant topics and, at times, be "evocative" in terms of posing questions to encourage participation. The skillful leader must be careful not to dominate the group and must direct his/her behavior toward teaching the members to work effectively as a group and relate to one another in a constructive manner. Thus, the leader may assume many roles within the group (e.g., listener, advisor, empathizer, blocker, etc.).

It may appear that becoming an effective leader of an anger control program for adolescents is an overwhelming task that requires a tremendous amount of training and experience. However, if leaders (such as childcare workers, counselors, nurses, involved parents, probation officers, psychiatrists, psychologists, social workers, teachers, therapists, etc.) present the anger control training in a systematic, structured manner, the training itself becomes a rewarding learning experience. In our opinion, the only prerequisite characteristics should be commitment, enthusiasm, interest, and motivation to learn how to teach angry, aggressive, acting-out adolescents how to gain control over their behavior.

Group Leaders as Cotherapists

Leaders of adolescent anger control groups work much more effectively as cotherapists than as solo therapists for several reasons. Cotherapists increase group members' involvement in terms of their active participation in group tasks and processes. They tend to complement and support one another's style, thus making the task of leading a group much less demanding and much more enjoyable. Cotherapists can be extremely flexible in the roles that they assume and can share a number of responsibilities. One therapist can be task-oriented while the other can be process-oriented; when one leader is concentrating on or involved in a particular interaction, the other leader can direct his/her attention to other members to observe signs of stress, noninvolvement, or potential participation. Together they can serve as models for giving both positive and negative messages, comfortably agreeing or disagreeing with each other without destructive competition. As coleaders, their range of observational and problem-solving capabilities is greater, thus enhancing their ability to troubleshoot members' resistance and/or noncompliance. For the novice therapist, being paired with an experienced therapist can be a tremendous learning experience and a great anxiety reducer. Finally, following group meetings, cotherapists can provide valuable feedback to one another concerning each other's behavior during the group meeting.

Anger Control Training for Group Leaders

The following comprehensive group anger control training approach for professionals is strongly recommended. First, we suggest that professionals participate in a series of seminars or workshops conducted by those experienced in running anger control stress inoculation groups. This training experience can vary in length and format and should include booster and follow-up workshops. Such a training experience will afford professionals the opportunity to learn cognitive-behavioral techniques tailored to help them deal with both their own job-related stress and anger (frequently referred to as "burnout") and the anger/aggression related problems of the adolescents with whom they work directly. Used in anger control training is the Stress Inoculation Training (SIT) approach which is a self-regulatory, coping skills approach with special emphasis on the cognitive components of anger. Adolescents are encouraged to moderate, regulate, and prevent out-of-control anger and aggression and to implement problem-solving action in response to provocation. The effectiveness of the SIT model has been demonstrated in the fields of stress, pain, and anger management (Meichenbaum & Cameron, 1972; Meichenbaum & Jaremko, 1983; Novaco, 1975, 1979, 1980; Turk, 1974). This approach has been applied to adolescents exhibiting anger-control problems (Feindler et al., 1984b, 1986; Schlicter & Horan, 1981; Schrader et al., 1977; Spirito et al., 1981) as well. The SIT model includes the following training goals and phases based on Novaco's 1975 intervention program.

OVERVIEW OF GROUP ANGER
CONTROL TRAINING

Goals

Prevention

The focus of this goal is on reducing the frequency of angry, aggressive outbursts adolescents might exhibit on a week-to-week basis. When conducting anger control discussions, professionals are encouraged to prompt adolescents to question whether they needed to get angry in the first place and whether acting out served any function of resolving the conflict. The key therapeutic aspect for professionals is to encourage adolescents not to get angry when their anger serves no positive function.

Regulation

Since the expression of anger occurs along two dimensions, intensity and duration, the focus of this goal is twofold. First, adolescents are helped to understand that when their anger becomes extreme or out of hand, they are wasting personal power, energy, and time. Uncontrolled anger can create an emotional imbalance that may disrupt composure, concentration, and poise and interfere with performance potential on a personal and social level. "Keeping their cool"—or regulating the intensity of their anger—can spell the difference between failure and success.

Second, since adolescents typically tend to be preoccupied and ruminate on negative thoughts concerning an anger-provoking situation, the duration of the anger cycle tends to be prolonged. The second focus is on interrupting the adolescent's preoccupation early in the anger cycle or chain and on providing alternative cognitive activity (e.g., anger-control, task-oriented self-instructions) that will enable them to feel and act in a more adaptive manner in anger-provoking situations.

Execution

This goal focuses on providing the adolescents with skills for appropriately expressing their anger. Many adolescents who lose control or act out do so because they have no effective ways of dealing with or expressing their anger in a direct, appropriate manner. In fact, aggressive youths often vent their frustrations, anger, and aggression indirectly at people and objects. In special educational programs, group homes, residential schools, court-related facilities, children's psychiatric hospitals, foster homes, outpatient treatment agencies, and a variety of other placements for youth, acting-out behaviors at times can run rampant. Such youthful out-of-control anger and aggression creates a great deal of job-related stress for professionals at one time or another. By providing adolescents who lose control of their anger with more appropriate, direct, socially acceptable ways of dealing with and expressing their feelings, stress and anger will be under control not only for them, but also for the rest of us! Thus, the executional goal is to teach adolescents how to nonverbally and verbally respond to anger provocation more constructively.

In summary, group anger control training is designed to help adolescents develop self-management skills and reduce occurrences of chronic acting-out episodes. The stress inoculation approach to adolescent anger management is tailored to provide anger control skills that are preventative, regulatory, and executional in nature and purpose. By helping adolescents self-manage the undesirable cognitive-physiological-behavioral patterns of their anger experience and by providing them with more positive alternative ways to think, feel, and act in the face of provocation, professionals will then be able to allocate more time to teaching adolescents other valuable skills.

Stress Inoculation Group Anger Control Training Phases

The stress inoculation approach to adolescent anger management involves three training phases. Although these phases will be presented here in a successive fashion, they are actually interrelated on a session-to-session basis during implementation. Furthermore, these three training phases will offer adolescents a set of self-control skills that will permit them to gradually cope more effectively with the cognitive, physiological, behavioral, and environmental stressors encountered in their daily lives.

Educational/Cognitive Preparation Phase

The goal of this phase is to teach adolescents to be experts in terms of understanding their own personal anger patterns. Group leaders can achieve this goal by meeting the following objectives.

1. Leaders should establish and maintain a therapeutic working relationship with group members and significant others who work directly with them throughout their group anger control program. We cannot overemphasize the importance of this relationship; a successful group experience will be mediated and positive change will be facilitated by a relationship between group leaders, group members, and their significant others that is characterized by mutual trust, warmth, empathic understanding, support, and acceptance.

2. They should educate adolescent group members about how their out-of-control anger occurs in terms of the interaction between cognitive, physiological, and behavioral components.

3. Leaders should educate adolescent group members about the situational antecedents that trigger or ignite their out-of-control anger and how to use these antecedent cues as triggers to "chill out."

4. They should teach adolescents how to discriminate between positive and negative reactions to provocation. Emphasis is placed on encouraging adolescent members to use more adaptive ways of responding to anger provocation by introducing cognitive-behavioral anger control techniques that they can use to cope more effectively with daily stress and conflict.

These objectives are accomplished through adolescent members' discussion, self-assessment, and self-monitoring of conflict situations.

Skill Acquisition Phase

The goal of this phase is to teach adolescents cognitive-behavioral techniques that they can use to cope more effectively with anger-provoking situations. In order for the reader to acquire a concise overview of the component skills in this phase, they will be classified in two distinct categories (as recommended by Novaco, 1979).

Cognitive Component Skills Training. At this level of training, group leaders provide adolescents with cognitive coping strategies that are tailored to do the following:

1. Cue adolescents for anger provocation by training them to use their attentional skills to prepare for possible provocation before it happens and by helping them identify potential "triggers."

2. Alter adolescents' views of anger provocation in terms of the exaggerated importance they sometimes attach to such events by prompting them to identify, challenge, and moderate their irrational thoughts. Members will be trained to conduct a cognitive assessment of those negative thoughts that lead to loss of control and will be provided with thought-stopping techniques that will give them the time needed to restructure their intense, angry, and negative thoughts into something more adaptive and positive.

3. Let adolescents use their "private speech" (self-instructions) to prepare, guide, and direct them in a controlled manner through anger provocations. Members will also use these self-instructional capabilities to reflect later on resolved and unresolved conflicts in terms of how they handled their anger.

Behavioral Component Skills Training. At this level of training, group leaders provide adolescents with behavioral coping strategies that are tailored to do the following:

1. Moderate adolescents' physiological anger arousal by providing them with skills training in relaxation.

2. Direct adolescents to be more effective in communicating their anger verbally and nonverbally by providing them with training in acting assertively rather than aggressively in the face of provocation.

3. Organize the manner in which adolescents solve their anger-related problems by providing them with systematic training in problem solving. Leaders will teach members to objectively define the problems, enumerate alternative responses, list consequences for each response and rank order alternatives, implement an alternative, and evaluate the outcome.

4. Work through, by utilizing modeling and behavioral rehearsal formats, the proper timing sequences and conditions that will enhance the effective use of the various cognitive-behavioral anger control skills.

5. Negotiate a commitment through contracting techniques to begin using their newly learned anger control skills outside of their group training experience in order to promote generalization to other settings.

The reader should note the C-A-L-M D-O-W-N acronym.

Skill Application Phase

The goal of this phase is to expose adolescents to graduated, stressful anger-provoking situations and teach them how to apply anger control skills to simulated role-plays and then to real-life situations. Leaders can achieve this goal by focusing their efforts on the following:

1. Through group discussion of members' past conflicts, leaders and members can rehearse appropriate anger control skills to graduated provoking stressors via role reversals (e.g., members initially play the role of the provoker, leaders play the adolescent modeling proper timing and sequencing of anger-control skills, followed by individual roles reversed).

2. By viewing videotaped films that model negatively and positively executed anger-control skills, members will be able to observe and identify the "right" and "wrong" approach to anger control. Following the viewing of these film clips, members can then role play similar situations with group leaders and other members. These role plays can be videotaped and replayed for coaching and feedback purposes.

3. Adolescent graduates of past programs can serve as guest peer models in order to coach, model, and rehearse with members who are having difficulty mastering the proper timing and sequencing of skills during simulated role-play practices. Adolescent anger control graduates can also be used as helpers outside of the group situation and prompt members to use their skills in daily real-life provoking situations.

4. The use of preplanned barbs (Kaufmann & Wagner, 1972) in group training situations (delivered first by leaders, then by graduates) will enhance members' skill application capabilities. Gradually, when members demonstrate skill competency in group training sessions, preplanned and unplanned barbs can be delivered outside of the training situation by significant others (e.g., childcare workers, nurses, teachers, psychiatrists, involved parents, etc.) who work directly with the adolescent.

5. Assigning adolescents written homework that requires them to record and have verified (by significant other's signature) their use of anger control skills in provoking situations occurring outside of the training situation will also enhance their skill application across settings.

In summary, stress inoculation group anger control training consists of interrelated training phases and goals that are designed to help adolescents acquire a repertoire of more effective skills for managing stressful, anger-provoking situations. The first training phase educates adolescents about the interaction between the cognitive, physiological, and behavioral components of their anger experience, the adaptive and maladaptive functions of their anger, the situational triggers that provoke their anger, and the skills that they can use to gain better self-control over their anger. During the second training phase, adolescents learn specific cognitive-behavioral coping skills that are then practiced in increasingly stressful, anger-provoking situations. This gradual exposure of members to stressful, provoking situations while helping them apply newly acquired skills is the focus of the third phase, the inoculation procedure that prepares adolescents to cope successfully with similar provoking situations outside of group sessions. Thus, these training conditions teach adolescents to prepare for triggers that have the potential to provoke their anger, to substitute self-instructions, relaxation, assertion and problem-solving skills as mediating responses between the situational trigger and their previously out-of-control anger response, and to practice these alternative responses during increasingly stressful, anger-provoking situations.

ADDITIONAL TRAINING
GUIDELINES AND TECHNIQUES

In addition to receiving training in the anger control SIT model, we strongly recommend that group leaders receive concurrent training in the following techniques. These methods can be used in any type of adolescent group training program.

The Group Leader's Teaching Philosophy

Interactions occurring in adolescent groups sometimes resemble an extension or reenactment of family interactions or experiences. Leaders of adolescent groups thus have an excellent opportunity to assume a teaching-parent role (cf. Fixen, Phillips, Dowd, & Palma, 1981; Phillips, Phillips, Fixen, & Wolf, 1974), a demanding yet very rewarding experience. This role requires a great deal of patience, understanding, and commitment to direct, guide, and teach adolescents the prosocial coping skills needed to function as autonomous members of society. Finally, teaching-parent leaders serve as advocates for youths participating in their groups by teaching them how to make decisions that are in their best interests, both personally and socially.

The Group Leader's Teaching Skills

Active Listening

Of all the requisite skills for effective teaching and training, we consider the ability to actively listen the most important. Good active listening enables the leader to more accurately identify the nature of the member's problems and the circumstances that may influence their behavior patterns. These, in turn, provide a severity measure of the problem, which can serve as a baseline against which results of training programs can be compared. In addition, active listening skills help leaders become more aware of their own reactions to adolescents' problems and how their reactions might be affecting such problems.

We strongly recommend that leaders use the following four active listening skills (Cormier & Cormier, 1979).

1. *Clarification* begins with a questioning probe such as, "do you mean that. . . " or "are you saying that . . . " and ends with a rephrasing of the speaker's statement. The clarification is used by the leader to determine if the message was accurately heard and received.

2. *Paraphrase* is an active listening skill that requires the leader to restate or rephrase in his/her own words the content of the message. The paraphrase is used to cue speakers to focus on the objective material (e.g., references to specific situations, people, objects, or ideas) contained in their messages, rather than to focus on or attend to the subjective material (e.g., feelings), which could be anger inducing.

3. *Reflection* requires the leader to restate in his/her own words the feeling component of the adolescent's message. Reflection is a skill used by the leader to help speakers become more aware of the type of feelings that they are experiencing.

4. *Summarization* is an active listening skill that requires the leader to sum up both the content and feeling components of the speaker's message. This ties all messages together by combining paraphrases and reflections to identify a common theme or cognitive-affective-behavioral pattern.

Basically, group leaders' active listening skills will serve as a powerful teaching method. Members, as well as their significant others, will be assisted in talking more about their concerns, thoughts, feelings, and actions.

Shaping

Shaping is a technique that will provide leaders the opportunity to begin working with adolescents at their present skill level. It is designed to motivate the adolescent to perform new behaviors by initially reinforcing behaviors already in his/her skill repertoire. Shaping new behaviors requires that the leader provide reinforcement for successive approximations, or slight changes in the adolescent's behavior, which gradually resemble the targeted goal behavior. Remember, shaping means reinforcing *improvement* , or reinforcing the adolescent for gradually exhibiting better behavior.

It is critical for group leaders to make this learning process a positive one for the adolescent. That means leaders need to reinforce members for improvement, rather than for absolute performance. In order to insure that the member experiences more successes than failures, be sure to reinforce the adolescent for:

1. exhibiting an approximation to or component of the target behavior
2. increases in accuracy
3. increases in effort or participation
4. increases in time spent performing the targeted behavior.

During this learning process, if the adolescent begins to experience many failures, it will be necessary for the leader to determine whether the steps or approximations are too difficult. If so, the desired goal behavior needs to be broken down into smaller, easier to learn component steps. If the cause of failure is a result of moving too rapidly through the shaping process, the leader then needs to back up and reinforce the member for the previous step at which success was attained and break down future shaping steps into smaller, less demanding ones.

Reinforcement

Throughout our discussion of shaping we have frequently used the term *reinforcement*. For those who are not familiar with the terminology and philosophy of reinforcement theory, a brief review is offered. Reinforcement is the process by which the consequences that follow behavior influence the likelihood that the behavior will recur. When a behavior is followed by a positive consequence, the frequency of that behavior will increase (reinforcement). When a behavior is followed by a negative consequence, the frequency of that behavior will decrease (punishment). In many cases, behavior decreases if it is not reinforced soon after it occurs (extinction). Moreover, there are two types of reinforcers: positive and negative. A positive reinforcer is any consequence or event whose contingent presentation increases or maintains the likelihood that the behavior will recur (e.g., a reward). A negative reinforcer is any consequence or event whose contingent removal or withdrawal increases the likelihood that the behavior will occur again. Negative reinforcers are usually associated with the termination of a restriction, penalty, threat, or punishing event. It is important for leaders to remember that reinforcers are defined by their effect on the adolescent's behavior. What serves as a reinforcer for one member might not so serve for another.

Positive Reinforcement. To define potential positive reinforcers for the adolescents who have participated in our groups, we simply asked: "Since being here, what are some of the things you enjoy doing most?" or "If you could choose what you wanted to do during your free time, what would you do and who would you do it with?" The results of this investigation are listed in Table 3.1 by category of the reinforcers earned by adolescents who participated in our training groups.

The most powerful reinforcer leaders can deliver is social reinforcement. It has been our experience that a majority of our successfully trained adolescents thrive on social praise and approval. In fact, not only is social reinforcement effective in increasing appropriate prosocial behavior in adolescents, it is the best way for group leaders to establish and maintain a positive therapeutic working relationship with such youths. Leaders can work effectively with the angriest, most aggressive kids by delivering their attention in a contingent, systematic manner. Eimers and Aitchison (1977) developed a seven-step approach to teaching parents how to give effective social praise to their children. We have adapted and applied this approach in our group work, which is detailed in Table 3.2.

Table 3.1. Effective Reinforcers for Adolescents

Activity Reinforcers

> Trip to hospital canteen
> Go out to eat at a fast food restaurant
> Go out to eat at a nice restaurant
> Go shopping
> See a movie
> Go to a rock concert with favorite staff and/or friend
> Go for a drive
> Go for a walk with favorite staff and/or friend
> Engage in sports activity with favorite staff and/or friend
> Watch videos
> Watch break dance performances that are videotaped
> Be director of anger-control role plays that are videotaped
> Be an actor in anger-control role plays that are videotaped
> Listen to Walkman
> Play cards with favorite staff and peers
> Have special meal brought in to share with favorite staff and/or friend
> Have a pizza party
> Go out for ice cream
> Play video games
> Go out to pet store
> Go to park
> Visit a favorite staff or friend on another living unit
> Be allowed to stay up a little later than others

Social Reinforcers

> Group leaders and other staff actively listening
> Student of the Week Award announcements
> Positive facial expression such as smile, wink, affirmative nod of the head
> Positive physical contact such as high five, handshake, hug, touch, pat on back or shoulder
> Clicking of fingers
> Verbal praise
> Acceptance into group
> Graduating from group
> Display of graphs in terms of restriction reduction

Token Reinforcers

> Point system
> Student of the Week Award
> Earning checks on a chart during group sessions

Material Reinforcers

> Soda of choice
> Candy of choice
> "Chill-Out" T-shirts*

*We actually give "Chill-Out" T-shirts to graduates of our program.

Decreasing Maladaptive Behavior. Unfortunately, there will be occasions during group sessions in which adolescents test the leaders with annoying, sometimes persistent behaviors. These behaviors (e.g., whispering, indistinct body sounds, playful poking, name-calling or teasing, etc.) can undermine the group process and must be dealt with. We have found the most effective method of reducing or

Table 3.2. Seven-Step Approach to Social Reinforcement

Whenever adolescent members are displaying positive prosocial behaviors in or out of the group situation, leaders should deliver social praise in the following systematic manner.

1. Establish eye contact with the adolescent. Praise delivered without eye contact will reflect insecurity on the part of the leader.
2. Move as close to the adolescent as he/she will permit. There will be some adolescents who will resist or become uncomfortable with physical closeness. With these members, a distance ranging from 3 to 5 feet will suffice.
3. Maintain a positive facial expression. Smile and nod. Present positive body language and lean slightly forward. Snap or click fingers if possible. Finger snapping is a very quick and easy way to show a sign of applause and, it is a lot simpler than clapping your hands. Before using the finger snapping technique, remember to clarify what it means to group members.
4. Make several positive verbal comments to the adolescent. Be creative. Avoid using pat statements in a repetitious manner, such as, "good, John" or "thank you." Be descriptive in your praise and "own" your reaction, such "John, I really like it when you participate in group role plays."
5. In a similar vein, be sure to praise the behavior and not the adolescent. The goal is to get the member to discriminate between those behaviors which result in personal satisfaction and those which do not (e.g., "Mary, the assertion technique you selected for the particular conflict situation was a good one. Keep up the good work.").
6. Show physical affection to the adolescent whenever possible. Again, with some members this will be difficult. However, a quick handshake, a "high five," or a pat on the shoulder or back will make your social reinforcement that much more powerful.
7. Most importantly, praise should be delivered immediately after the desired behavior occurs.

eliminating these behaviors is ignoring, a form of extinction. Please refer to Table 3.3 for details of the five-step approach to ignoring developed by Eimers and Aitchison (1977).

Dealing with Aggressive Members. Adolescents who have anger control problems present a challenge, since they have the potential to become physically dangerous at any time. Their potential to lose control and become aggressive requires that group leaders be aware of sources of conflict that members could bring with them into the group situation. Possible sources of conflict for the adolescent could be:

- anger at having to be somewhere other than where they want to be
- anger over having failed at something
- anger that arose from prior interpersonal or group interactions or conflicts.

Table 3.3. Five-Step Approach to Ignoring

1. Be consistent. If you decide to ignore a particular behavior during group sessions, be sure to ignore it immediately and stick to your commitment to ignore.
2. While ignoring the behavior, maintain a neutral facial expression. Also, move slightly away from the adolescent (3 to 5 feet at least), and be sure to make no eye contact whatsoever while the annoying behavior is occurring.
3. Ignore the adolescent's verbal and nonverbal behavior while the annoying behavior is occurring.
4. Actively attend to all other group members who are displaying appropriate group behavior.
5. Immediately attend to the adolescent once the annoying behavior has ceased and he/she is displaying more active involvement.

If a group member is observed to be on the verge of losing control (e.g., displays increased physiological tension, physical closeness, verbal threats, angry stares and gestures, etc.), it is critical for the leader to intervene quickly to interrupt the conflict early in the anger chain. Physical intervention should be used only in those crisis situations in which the leader's nonverbal (e.g., staying in close proximity and touch control) and verbal calming techniques fail to deescalate the conflict (Randall, 1985). On such occasions, all group interactions should be temporarily stopped and agitated group members should be physically separated from the group and each other as safely and therapeutically as possible. One group leader and any available direct care staff should be responsible for gaining control of and escorting the agitated group members out of the group, while the other leader attends to the rest of the group. These remaining members should be guided through an objective assessment of the conflict situation just witnessed (e.g., "Let's take a look at what just happened. Anyone got any ideas about how it happened and what could have been done to prevent it?"). By getting members to examine the conflict from a therapeutic framework, participants will gain a clearer understanding of the circumstances that trigger such conflicts, as well as more adaptive methods of dealing with such triggers. As soon as possible following the session, group leaders should meet individually with the expelled members and review the conflict, using the conflict resolution "teaching interaction" approach (Fixen et al., 1981) described in Table 3.4.

Other Group Management Techniques. Although there is a variety of group therapy programs for adolescents, all involve as a goal the development of cohesiveness—the sharing of ideas, feelings, and experiences in an atmosphere of mutual respect and understanding. The therapeutic relevance of group cohesiveness has been well documented and is based on the fact that the more members are attracted to the group training program, the more they are influenced by its standards. Concurrently, the more cohesive the group is, the more effective it is in terms of inducing behavior change in its members.

Table 3.4. Conflict Resolution Teaching Interaction

1. Conduct an objective assessment of the conflict situation identifying triggers, inappropriate group behavior, resulting consequences, etc., so that the adolescent clearly understands what he/she did wrong in the group.
2. Provide the adolescent with several cognitive-behavioral coping alternatives to deal more effectively with conflicts in the future.
3. Do a comprehensive check. Ask the member to verbalize what was just recommended to make sure the recommendation for change was understood.
4. Prompt the adolescent to practice the recommended coping strategies in front of you. Provide coaching, feedback, and social reinforcement to enhance the quality of performance.
5. Encourage the adolescent to use anger control strategies when faced with similar conflicts in the future.
6. Provide adolescent with immediate social reinforcement whenever he/she is observed using recommended anger control skills.

Some of the techniques used to promote an atmosphere of unity of purpose and foster group cohesiveness can result in the development of social/interpersonal skills necessary for adaptive, congenial, and appropriate behavior not only within the group, but within all facets of the adolescent's life experience (e.g., family, work, school, etc.) as well.

The atmosphere of the first official group session is of great importance. If leaders can set a warm, friendly, relaxed, and accepting tone, the probability of the group beginning and continuing in a positive, helpful manner will be enhanced. Cohesiveness can also be facilitated in the first meeting by formulating a group contract between leaders and members that clearly states mutual expectations, commitment, and investments toward personal behavioral change.

To further enhance group cohesiveness and facilitate transfer and maintenance of acquired anger control skills, leaders must provide multiple opportunities for members to practice self-control coping behaviors under a variety of stimulus conditions. Initially, group leaders serve as facilitators by using selective prompts, cues, and reinforcement contingencies to shape desirable behaviors and extinguish maladaptive ones. As time elapses and group members exhibit an increased capability to take on more responsibility for behavior change, leaders must structure the transfer of control of contingencies to members. Group leaders can shape self-control skills by providing members with cues on how, what, and when it is appropriate to reinforce desirable behavior, then gradually fade these cues out. By providing the opportunity for members to learn how to reward each other for appropriate behavior, their dependency on the leader decreases at the same time as their independent functioning is enhanced.

To foster generalization, leaders should provide multiple opportunities for members to practice acquired anger control skills in situations that successively approximate real-life conditions. Once again, leaders must initially model the appropriate coping behaviors, but they may also use peer role models and a variety of modeling techniques to shape and facilitate skill acquisition.

Permitting members to formulate different types of contingency contracts (e.g., self-administered, cojoint, behavioral exchange) among each other will also optimize group cohesiveness as it provides the opportunity for increased member–member interaction.

How to Deal with Resistance. Gottman and Leiblum (1974) define resistance as occurring when group members are not meeting the leader's expectations regarding meaningful goal-oriented therapeutic work. There are several effective approaches to dealing with resistance. The selection of the approach depends greatly upon whether the resistance is due to subject variables (e.g., maladaptive cognitions or skill deficits) or interactional variables (e.g., communication problems in group situations). Regardless of the approach or method used, it is important for group leaders to remember to use a warm, friendly, relaxed, ınonthreatening posture and tone of voice in dealing with a member's resistance. Methods of dealing with resistance are addressed fully in Chapter 5.

Setting up the Group. What makes The Art of Self-Control program unique is that it is one of the few in the country that uses staff volunteers from different departments as filmed role models. The videotaped role plays depict typical anger-provoking situations in which hospital staff express their anger first in an inappropriate, aggressive manner, then in an appropriate, assertive manner, thus modeling the various anger control skills to be taught during group treatment sessions. Ideas for role plays came from the direct-care staff who worked directly with those youths referred to the training program.

In setting up anger control programs for adolescents, we strongly recommend the development and utilization of videotaped films. These films have several advantages over live modeling formats: They capture naturalistic modeling sequences that might be difficult to produce using live modeling; professionals developing the films can exercise greater control over the creation of modeling scenes; they permit the use of multiple models, repeated viewing of the same model, and reuse of the videotaped films with other adolescents. Finally, there is the added benefit of efficiency; this type of modeling format will reduce the amount of time group leaders will have to spend working with each adolescent individually (Thelen, Fry, Fehrenbach, & Frautschi, 1979).

Prior to beginning anger control training with adolescents, a brief program presentation to prospective group members is suggested. A brief showing of a modeling film clip displaying the "wrong" way of controlling anger is an effective way of increasing prospective members' curiosity about the training program. Selection of group members should be based on the degree of motivation they have to learn how to control their anger; their capacity to work together as a group; the severity of their anger control problems; and their commitment to participate in the program. The signing of a contract that defines the purpose, tasks, and goals of the program is beneficial. See Table 3.5 for an example of a group contract.

In residential settings, groups should meet twice a week for a 6-week period; in outpatient settings, once a week for a 12-week period is recommended. Length of sessions can range from 45 to 90 minutes, and the size of the group can range from 8 to 12 members. Table 3.6 lists various materials which are helpful in running group sessions.

In summary, The Art of Self Control anger control program provides adolescent participants training in relaxation, self-instructions, the use of coping statements, assertiveness, self-monitoring of anger and conflict incidents, and problem solving. Specific teaching strategies that enhance members' skill acquisition are live modeling, behavioral rehearsal and practice, negative and positive symbolic modeling videotaped films, role playing utilizing videotape equipment, videotape stop-gap feedback, and other visual aids such as cartoons and cue

Table 3.5. What The Art of Self-Control Program is All About

The goals of this program are:

> To help me learn to handle myself better in conflict situations.
> To help me not get so uptight when I am provol ed.
> To help me learn to get along better with people who set the rules.

What do I have to do for this program?

> I have to attend a half hour lesson every _____ and _____ at _____ for about 8 weeks.
> I have to keep records about my behavior during the day.
> I have to practice the things I am taught in the lessons and finish all homework.
> I have to role play during the lessons.

What will I get for being in this program?

> I'll have a chance to talk over the problems I'm having with others.
> I will be able to control myself much better and solve my own problems.
> At the end of each session, if I've done my homework and cooperated with the group leader, I'll earn a snack.
> At the end of the program if I have participated fully, I will be invited to a pizza party.

Witness: _____

cards. A point system for in-session compliance and participation provides participants the opportunity to earn end-of-session reinforcers, weekly reinforcers, and, at the termination of the training program, awards for outstanding individual mastery of anger control skills.

The following pages provide a session-by-session description of the 12-session Art of Self-Control group anger control program.

Table 3.6. Materials Needed for Group Sessions

1. Session manual and objectives checklist
2. Contract forms
3. Self-monitoring data sheets
4. Daily behavior graph forms
5. Videotape equipment
6. Student relaxation outline
7. Assessment devices (e.g., hassle logs, ABC's worksheets, and role-play rating scales) and physiological measures (e.g., finger temperature thermometers, stress dots, and temperature graphs)
8. Other student worksheets and cartoons
9. Other materials—blackboard, flash cue cards, props, role play scripts, handouts, 3 x 5 inch index cards, pencils
10. End of session reinforcers—cold soda or other favorite snacks

THE ART OF SELF-CONTROL:
A GROUP ANGER
CONTROL PROGRAM

Session 1

1. Explain the rationale for the training program:

   (a) To teach a variety of techniques that will assist the student in controlling his/her anger in provocative/conflict situations.
   (b) To increase personal power and stay out of the "Fool's Ring."*

   Examples of people with excellent self-control: Bruce Lee, Chris Evert Lloyd, Muhammed Ali, Mary Lou Retton, Nancy Lopez, Dave Winfield.

2. Define program rules:

   (a) Set up meeting times, length of program, length of sessions, how to participate (i.e., no interrupting).
   (b) Use behavioral contingencies: *In-session* checklist (Figure 3.1) for following instructions, staying on task, cooperation, doing homework assignments.
   (c) Introduce in-session checklist chart: ranges from 0–5 points per session. Reinforcers (sodas and candy bars) contingent upon in-session behaviors. Students must accumulate a minimum of 4 points to earn a reinforcer. Checklist includes: coming on time, handing in homework assignments, first 15 minutes of cooperation, second 15 minutes of cooperation, third 15 minutes of cooperation.
   (d) Institute end-of-program lottery: person(s) with most checks for each behavior will have the opportunity to win prizes (posters and records).
   (e) Ask students for summary of program rules.

3. Nature of training program:

   (a) Homework assignments will be given.
   (b) Participation in role plays using videotape equipment will be required.
   (c) Group discussions will be encouraged.

4. Introduce brief relaxation techniques:

   (a) Deep breaths: Explain to students that taking a few slow deep breaths can help in maintaining a controlled response to anger provocations. Give students examples of athletes who visibly use a few deep breaths before attempting some event (i.e., at the foul line, in the boxing ring, etc.). Remind students about their physiological cues and discuss how deep breathing would function to:
      • reduce physiological tension

*For further information on the "Fool in the Ring" paradigm, see pages 89–90.

- refocus their attention away from external provoking stimuli to internal control
- provide a time delay before making a choice of how to respond

(b) Backward counting and imagery: Present these techniques as additional methods for providing time delay and a refocusing of attention.

- Have students practice turning away from a provoking stimulus (do this via a spontaneous role play) and silently, starting with 20, count backwards with a slow, measured pace.
- Present a visual image that elicits a calming or pleasant state. Use sports analogies such as "float like a butterfly" or a cooling-down image such as "deep freeze." Allow students to generate their own visual images with a criterion that the image is a clear, nonverbal one.
- Be sure to describe effective timing of these additional responses and rehearse their implementation.

5. Give out session points and contingent reinforcers.

Session 2

1. Recap–Begin with a review of:

   (a) Rationale of program
   (b) Program rules
   (c) Brief relaxation techniques

2. Introduce hassle log:

   (a) Hand out hassle logs to students and ask someone different to read each item. If possible provide a large visual example of the data sheet.

FIGURE 3.1. Point checklist for anger control session

Name	On Time	Handed in Homework	Cooperation

Session No.: ____   Date: ____

Comments:

(b) Run through an example of a hypothetical conflict with students and demonstrate how to fill out the hassle log.

(c) Give rationale for using hassle logs: It is a self-monitoring device that will provide each student with an accurate picture of how they handled conflict situations during the week. It is a learning device for students regarding what sets them off and is an opportunity to report situations that were different and that were handled well. Finally, it provides scripts for in-session role plays. Explain to each student the contingency: that if they complete a hassle sheet appropriately, then it will be used as a script for videotaped role plays. Students completing said contingency will be able to be "actors."

(d) Consequences for student not completing hassle log: He/she will not earn points and thus jeopardize his/her chance of receiving reinforcers. Also will not be able to participate as an actor in the videotaping of role plays.

3. Behavioral interviewing and some initial history taking on how students handle conflicts/provocations:

(a) Give self examples.

(b) Ask students for specific conflict incidents that have occurred at or outside of setting (i.e., probe for prior confrontations with authority figures from schools or communities).

(c) Prompt students to enumerate *behaviors* ("What did you do?"), *consequences* ("What happened afterwards to you? To the other person?"), and *antecedents* ("What triggered the problem? What happened right before?").

4. Self-assessment of anger: Introduce the concept of A, B, C's (i.e., antecedents, actual behavior, consequences).

(a) Provoking stimulus — what gets the adolescent angriest. Situational variables are assessed in terms of what is going on in the environment (*overt* antecedents) and physiological states of fatigue, hunger, etc. (*covert* antecedents).

(b) Actual behavior/reaction: How do you know when you're angry? Focus on cognitive or physiological covert or overt cues that occur:
  • negative statements to self or with intention to harm the other person
  • physiological cues: "getting hot," muscle tension, rigid posture, angry stare, butterflies in stomach, hands clenched, facial muscles tensed, etc.

(c) Consequences: Ask students: "What happened to you as a result of not controlling your anger? Did you get into trouble?"

(d) Role plays: Training staff will demonstrate the components and an analysis of the feelings (covert and overt) prior to provocations.

- Use stop-gap method during role plays to help students tune into these overt and covert cues.

5. Summarize:

(a) Hassle log requirements: Present mechanics of completing hassle logs (where sheets will be located, best time to fill them out, what to do with completed data sheet).
(b) Tell students to tune into both overt and covert anger antecedents.
(c) Give out session points and contingent reinforcers.

Session 3

1. Collect and review homework assignments.
2. Recap. Begin with a review of A, B, C's as they relate to poor self-control:

(a) Provide distinctions between overt and covert cues of anger and aggression, asking students: "How do you know when you are angry? How do you know when another person is angry?" Have group members identify both internal (physiological or cognitive/self-statements) and external (observable motoric behavior) *cues* or antecedents to anger.
(b) Optional: Use examples from students' hassle logs and prompt them to identify the A, B, C's of a given anger-provoking situation.

3. Introduce the concept of *triggers*, which is the identification of the anger provoking antecedent event. In this discussion, focus on the beginning of the anger/aggression sequence. Prompt group members to identify things that trigger an anger cue in them. Define and focus on:

(a) Direct Triggers: Direct aversive provocations by another person. These may be in verbal (being told what to do) or nonverbal form (a kick, push, obscene gesture, etc.). Help group members identify patterns of provoking stimuli by asking questions such as: "Who are the people who trigger an anger response, and what do they do?"
(b) Indirect Triggers: These aversive stimuli include misperceptions or misattribution of events such as feeling blamed or feeling like someone is disapproving of them. Most of these events involve a faulty appraisal of what is going on, such as: "It's raining because I'm in a bad mood," or "He put me on restriction because he doesn't like me."
(c) Conduct several role plays (using students hassle logs) in order to aid in the identification of triggers. These might include:
- sports analogies, such as when someone is deliberately tripped-up on the court or is not selected for a team.
- a peer getting in trouble for something he did not do.
- thinking a peer or adult is lying in regard to something promised to the adolescent.

(d) Prompt students to identify the cognitive self-statements made in relation to these direct and indirect triggers. Model and emphasize how these internal dialogues can increase anger out of proportion. Negative self-statements, especially misperceptions or misattributions, are the most sure-fire way of making a "mountain out of a molehill."

4. Introduce progressive relaxation:

   (a) Have students get as comfortable as possible.
   (b) Instruct them to only tense one muscle group at a time.
   (c) Tell them to only tense muscles 70–80% capacity; if they experience pain while tensing a given muscle, they should stop immediately.
   (d) Have students tense muscles for a time period of no longer than 10 seconds and then relax for 10–15 seconds.
   (e) Follow the suggested order of muscle groups for relaxation training presented in Table 3.7.
   (f) Discuss rationale for relaxation training.

5. Summarize:

   (a) Antecedent triggers and internal anger cues.
   (b) Hand out additional hassle logs.
   (c) Give out session points and contingent reinforcers.

Session 4

1. Review:

   (a) Triggers: both direct and indirect provoking stimuli.
   (b) Hassle logs: Have students briefly retell their conflict situations. Prompt them to identify antecedent cues and any situational triggers.

Table 3.7. Order of Muscle Groups for Relaxation Training

1. Clench right fist (hand and forearm)
2. Clench left fist (hand and forearm)
3. Clench both fists (hands, forearms)
4. Bend both elbows (biceps)
5. Frown (forehead, scalp)
6. Squint eyes (eye muscles, face)
7. Clench teeth (jaws)
8. Push back head (neck)
9. Shrug shoulders (shoulders and back)
10. Take a deep breath, hold and push (chest)
11. Tense stomach muscles as if you were preparing for a blow to the stomach
12. Tense buttocks and thighs by extending legs straight out, curling feet upward, pushing buttocks muscles downward
13. Tense legs/calf muscles by extending legs straight out and curling feet downward
14. Point toes forward (foot muscles)
15. Take a deep breath, hold and push, as you exhale, say "relax" to yourself and notice how the relaxation increases
16. Repeat sequence

2. Asserting adolescent rights: Conduct a discussion about adolescent rights with regard to rules/laws and authority figures in family, school community, and residential agencies.

(a) Ask group members to generate a list of rights, things to which they feel they are entitled. These might include:
  - I have the right to be listened to.
  - I have the right to explain my side of the story before any judgment is passed.
  - I have the right to my own property.

(b) Further this discussion by prompting a listing of the rights of others in their unit, school, etc. (include both peer and adult rights). *Stress* the importance of treating others like you would like to be treated.

(c) Distinguish between passivity, assertion, and aggression by providing students with a continuum of responses to these rights (use "fool in the ring" example cited in chapter 4).
  - passive—letting someone take away your rights
  - assertive—standing up for your rights but at the same time respecting other person's rights
  - aggressive—demanding your rights with no regard for the other person's rights

(d) Discuss the concept of peer pressure or coercion, which is often exerted to get another person to give up their rights. Discuss how peer pressure works, how to discriminate between your own needs/wants and group goals.

3. Introduce assertion techniques as alternative responses to aggression: Instruct group members to use these assertion techniques in response to provoking stimuli that require action. These responses are designed to deescalate conflict situations while maintaining rights and an appropriate level of self-control.

(a) Broken record: This response involves a calm, monotone repetition of what you want, e.g., "Please give me my radio back." The student is trained to continue to repeat the response in the same calm manner until the property is returned. There is no escalation in terms of increased voice volume, threatening gestures, etc.

(b) Empathic assertion: This is a form of assertion that involves a sensitive listening on the student's part to the other person's feeling state. Particularly useful when dealing with authority figures who are angry. For example:

> *Childcare staff:* "This room is a mess. I can't believe you guys are such slobs. Start cleaning immediately."
> *Student:* "I know you're upset with the mess, but we just got back from the rec room and haven't had time to clean up yet."

Discuss how the childcare staff in the above example would have felt better because his/her feelings were heard.

(c) Escalating assertion: This is a sequence of responses that increases in assertiveness in order to obtain a desired outcome. Begin with a minimal assertive response (MAR) and escalate to final contract option (FCO) in which a threat to the other person for noncompliance to original demand is presented. For example:

> 1st MAR = "Please return my radio."
> 2nd = "I asked you to return my radio."
> 3rd = "I want my radio now."
> 4th FCO = "If you don't give me my radio now, I will go tell staff and they will come and get my radio for me."

(d) Fogging: This is a technique used to short-circuit an aggressive verbal conflict by confusing the provoker with an agreement. For example:

> Provoker: "You are stupid."
> Target Student: "You're right, I am stupid."

Explain to group members that such an agreement does not indicate truth, but rather a way to turn things into a joke.

4. Show the videotape of inappropriate/appropriate versions of these assertion techniques, using the stop-gap method, which will allow students to identify the techniques.

5. Summarize:

(a) Discuss with students *when* to use assertive responses rather than withdrawal or aggressive responses. Assertion is optimal when the adolescent is certain of his/her rights in a situation and when there is a high probability of a nonaggressive, successful outcome to the problem situation.

(b) Review probable responses of others when the target student uses an assertive response—those situations or occasions when others will increase their aggression. Suggest to students ways of handling this increased aggression. Calm persistence is usually best, especially if you are certain of your requests/rights.

(c) Give out more hassle logs and instruct continued self-monitoring of conflict situations in which the anger control techniques taught so far (e.g., deep breathing, backward counting, imagery, and assertion responses) are used.

(d) Give out session points and contingency reinforcers and provide students with positive feedback concerning their cooperation and commitment.

Session 5

1. Recap with a review of the four assertion techniques:

   (a) Broken record
   (b) Empathic assertion
   (c) Escalating assertion
   (d) Fogging

2. Have students role play several conflict situations from their hassle logs utilizing the various assertion techniques. These role plays by students should be videotaped and played back to them for appropriate feedback.

3. Review with students *when* to use assertive responses rather than withdrawal or aggressive responses.

4. Hand out more hassle logs and continue encouraging group members to try and resolve conflict situations by using the anger control techniques taught so far (e.g., relaxation and assertion techniques).

5. Give out session points and contingent reinforcers to students.

Session 6

1. Review:

   (a) Four assertion techniques: broken record, empathic assertion, escalating assertion, and fogging.
   (b) Hassle log: Prompt students to tell what self-control techniques they used during the week to control their anger or resolve conflict situations. Provide social reinforcement for resolved conflicts using any of the techniques taught so far.

2. Reminders: Introduction of self-instruction training.

   (a) Define *reminders* as things we say to ourselves to guide our behavior or to get us to remember certain things. Ask group members to think of specific things they say to remind themselves to bring certain items to class, etc.
   (b) Give examples of situations where reminders (self-instruction) can be used in pressure situations, such as at the foul line during a very close basketball game and other sports examples.
   (c) Describe how reminders can also be helpful in situations in which the adolescent has to try hard to keep very calm.
   (d) Have group members generate a list of reminders that they use in those pressure-type situations. Write these on a large chart or blackboard for all to see. Some possible self-instructions include:
      • "Slow down."
      • "Take it easy."

- "Take a deep breath."
- "Cool it."
- "Chill out."
- "Ignore this."

3. Show the videotape of inappropriate/appropriate versions of using reminders, utilizing the stop-gap method, which will allow students to identify the various ways in which reminders can be used.

4. Homework Assignment: Give each group member an index card and instruct them to write down three reminders that "fit" for them. Instruct students to bring these cards to the next session, when they will be implemented during the videotaping of role plays.

5. Hand out session points and contingency reinforcers to students.

Session 7

Continuation of Self-Instruction Training

1. Review the rationale for using reminders: things we say to ourselves to guide our behavior or to get us to remember certain things.

2. Application of reminders procedure: Demonstrate the appropriate use of self-instructions to guide behavior in conflict or anger-producing situations.

(a) Overt to covert: Using a group member's hassle log as a script, model the use of overt reminders. Role play a situation in which one student is cursing out another, who is emitting audible reminders in order to ignore this behavior. Suggest the use of reminders *instead* of reacting to the direct provocation.

(b) Fully describe the substitution procedure, whereby a youth has a choice after recognizing the antecedent anger trigger. He/she can either react in an angry or aggressive way, which may lead to receipt of negative consequences *or* he/she can emit covert reminders to remain calm and uninvolved in the conflict situation.

(c) Demonstrate use of covert reminders, and review rationale for maintaining this level of self-control.

(d) Conduct role plays for all students who completed hassle logs. Prompt students to use the reminders listed on their index cards during the videotaping of role plays.
   - Emphasize that the *timing* of reminders is critical. Give examples of someone who uses reminders before any actual provocation (too soon) and after he/she has received a punishment for explosive behavior (too late).
   - Prompt adolescents to identify the time that is just right for emitting covert self-instructions.

(e) Play back videotape scenes and structure group members' responses to analyze:
- use of reminders, either overt or covert
- timing of reminders
- effectiveness of appropriate use of reminders

3. Hand out additional hassle logs and instruct students to continue using the various anger control techniques taught so far (relaxation, assertion, and reminders) in resolving conflict or anger-provoking situations.

4. Give out session points and contingency reinforcers and provide students with positive feedback concerning their cooperation and commitment.

Session 8

1. Review anger control techniques taught so far:

(a) Brief relaxation techniques: deep breaths, backward counting, and imagery/pleasant scene.
(b) Progressive relaxation: tensing and relaxing antagonistic muscle groups.
(c) Assertion techniques: broken record, fogging, empathic (friendly), and escalating assertion.
(d) Self-instruction training: reminders (overt to covert).

2. Collect hassle log and prompt students to identify what anger control technique they used to resolve conflict- or anger-provoking situations.

3. Introduce thinking-ahead procedure as another self-control technique to use in conflict or anger-provoking situations. Discuss results.

(a) Define thinking ahead as using problem solving and self-instructions to estimate future negative consequences for a current aggressive response to a conflict situation.
(b) Explain thinking-ahead procedure using the following contingency statement: "If I (*misbehavior*) now, then I will (*future negative consequence*)." Stress the importance of using future negative consequences as a reminder to not get involved in acting-out behavior and of appropriate timing in using the thinking-ahead procedure.

4. Show the videotape of appropriate/inappropriate versions of using thinking-ahead procedures. Use the stop-gap method, which will allow group members to identify the various ways in which the thinking-ahead procedure can be used.

5. Review behaviors that lead to loss of control, such as acting before thinking things out.

(a) Have students identify external and internal consequences for acting-out behavior (e.g., restrictions, feeling irritated and upset). Be sure to

prompt identification of both long-term and short-term negative consequences, internal and external punishers, and subtle social negative
consequences.

(b) Have students brainstorm long- and short-term negative consequences
for acting out (e.g., jail or restrictions). List these consequences in a
hierarchial manner on a blackboard or a large chart from least to most
aversive/undesirable.

(c) Field any questions the students might have concerning the thinking-
ahead procedure.

6. Give out session points and contingency reinforcers to students.

Session 9

Continuation of Thinking-Ahead Training
1. Review:

(a) Thinking-ahead procedure: Use of anticipated negative consequences
as a reminder to control anger and aggressive responses.

(b) To further explain the thinking-ahead process, use the contingency
statement: "If I (*misbehave*) now, then I will (*future negative consequence*)." Have students verbally rehearse this contingency statement.

2. Application of thinking-ahead procedure: Demonstrate the appropriate use
of thinking ahead to guide behavior in conflict or anger-provoking situations.

(a) Using videotape equipment, have students who completed their hassle
logs role play the thinking-ahead procedure.

(b) Focus on overt and covert consequences. Example:
• *Covert:* People not liking you, not trusting you, losing your friends.
• *Overt:* Having your privileges removed or being placed in a more
restricted environment.

(c) Play back videotaped scenes and structure group members' responses to
analyze if the students in a particular role play:
• *reminded* self of negative consequences
• *stopped* the possible misbehavior
• *substituted* an alternative behavior such as brief relaxation, assertion, reminders, ignored, etc.

3. Summarize:

(a) Briefly quiz students to determine if they understand the thinking-
ahead procedure.

(b) Have each student identify negative consequences that might occur in
the future that he/she can use to control his/her present behavior.

Instruct students to implement this technique in the coming weeks.

(c) Hand out more hassle logs and instruct students to continue monitoring conflict situations.

(d) Give out session points and contingency reinforcers.

Session 10

1. Review:

    (a) Prompt students to name and describe anger control techniques taught so far: brief relaxation, assertion, reminders, and thinking ahead.

    (b) Using videotape equipment, have students who have completed their hassle logs role play an anger control technique of their choice.

2. Introduce self-evaluation process:

    (a) Define self-evaluation as a method of providing oneself with feedback on how a conflict situation was handled. Basically, these self-evaluation responses are reminders that occur after a conflict situation to provide the individual with immediate feedback on behavior and feelings during a conflict.

    (b) Have students review hassle logs, placing emphasis on how they handled themselves (recognize subtleties between handling a situation "great" or "just OK"). Prompt students to identify their current repertoire of self-statements for conflicts handled well and conflicts handled poorly.

    (c) Utilizing hassle logs, focus on coping statements used by students before, during, and after conflict situations.
    - Focus on whether self-evaluative statement is reinforcing or punishing, regardless of whether the conflict situation was resolved or unresolved.
    - Define self-evaluation as another reminder that can guide personal behavior.
    - Provide examples of positive and negative self-evaluation statements. Trainers can provide examples of their own internal self-statements that serve either to reinforce or punish behavior. Definitions of self-reinforcers or punishers may be necessary.
    - Review internal cues (physiological and cognitive) to self-evaluation statements.
    - Model positive/reinforcing self-evaluation statements.
    - Give sequential example of coping statements used before, during, and after provocation.
    - Provide examples of reflective self-statements that control subsequent behavior in unresolved and resolved conflict situations.

- Prompt students to generate a group list of coping statements or corrective feedback responses that can be used after they have failed to control themselves in a conflict situation.
- Prompt group members to think about how they will change their behavior the next time they are in a conflict.

3. Summarize:

   (a) Review rationale for using self-evaluative statements (i.e., to guide future behavior).
   (b) Hand out more hassle logs.
   (c) Give out session points and contingency reinforcers.
   (d) Provide feedback to group participants on their continued cooperation and enthusiasm during group meetings and on any behavior changes that have been noted.

Session 11

1. Review:

   (a) Anger control techniques taught so far: brief relaxation, assertion, reminders, thinking ahead, etc.
   (b) Rationale for using self-evaluation statements, which are reminders used after a conflict situation to provide the individual with immediate feedback on behavior and feelings during a conflict. Define self-evaluation as another reminder that serves to guide personal behavior.

2. Problem-solving training: Making choices between anger control alternatives. A problem-solving sequence is outlined that will facilitate the choice of which technique to implement in which conflict situation. Present the following sequence to students on a large visual chart or blackboard and review each step, giving examples from the hassle logs they have presented in this session.

   (a) Problem definition: "What is the problem?" Prompt students to identify the antecedent stimuli, including provoking stimulus, situational variables, and internal anger cues. Combine all of these components into a clear problem statement. Example:
      - A student is accused of stealing money or clothing from another student. The problem definition is that the student must respond in a nonaggressive manner to an unfair accusation without receiving any negative consequences.

   (b) Generation of alternative solutions (Phase 2): "What can I do?" This phase requires individuals to brainstorm all of the possible responses to the problem situation. The process of brainstorming precludes the evaluation or critique of any responses generated until a later time. Prompt students to identify as many responses as possible for the above situation or any situation that they have described. Allow for creative and expansive problem-solution generation.

(c) Consequent—Evaluation: "What will happen if. . . . " Using methods similar to those incorporated in the think-ahead procedure, ask students to identify the most probable consequences occurring subsequent to each of the responses in Phase 2. At this point, both positive and negative consequences should be charted for each response. Prompt students to provide both overt and covert consequences and long- and short-term ones.

(d) Choosing a problem solution: "What will I do?" Ask students to rank order all solutions generated according to the desirability/undesirability or severity of the consequences enumerated above. The solution that *optimizes* positive consequences, *minimizes* negative consequences, and solves the presenting problem is the one to implement first. Follow up on the stealing example mentioned previously, and aid students in identifying the best solution in their own hassle log problems.

(e) Feedback: "How did it work?" The final step in this problem-solving procedure involves the evaluation of the solution based on its effectiveness in solving the problem. Use of self-evaluation reminders should be prompted at this stage also. If the selected solution has not been effective, students should be prompted to move on to the second choice solution and follow the same procedure.

3. Summarize:

(a) Briefly review problem-solving sequence:
- What is the problem?
- What can I do?
- What will happen if. . . .
- What will I do?
- How did it work?

Instruct members to use this sequence in order to solve one problem (does not have to be anger related) during the next few days.

(b) Give out more hassle logs and instruct students to continue monitoring conflict situations.

(c) Give out session points and contingency reinforcers.

Session 12

Program Review
Review:

(a) Concept of A, B, C's.
- *Antecedents* are provoking stimuli. Overt antecedents are situa-

tional variables in one's environment that provoke anger. Covert antecedents are physiological states, such as fatigue.

- *Behavior* is the individual's actual reaction to the provoking stimuli, which can involve a variety of cognitive, physiological, overt, or covert responses.
- *Consequences* are events that happen as a result of controlling or not controlling anger. Consequences can either be rewarding or punishing.

(b) Concept of triggers—the provoking stimulus.
- Direct triggers are direct aversive provocations by another person. These may be in verbal or nonverbal form.
- Indirect triggers are the adolescent's misinterpretation or misattribution of events, which is the result of a faulty appraisal system. Indirect triggers may also include observed injustice or unfairness.

(c) Brief relaxation techniques: deep breaths, backward counting and imagery switching. Remind students about their physiological cues and how these techniques can be used to *reduce* tension and stress, *redirect* their attention away from external provoking stimuli to internal control, and *provide* a time delay before making a choice how to respond.

(d) Progressive relaxation (Jacobsen method):
- Guidelines: Tense one muscle group at a time; only tense muscles 70–80% capacity; if you experience any pain stop immediately; tense muscles for no longer than 10 seconds and then relax for 15–20 seconds.
- Order of muscle groups: hands and forearms, biceps, forehead and scalp, eye muscles and face, jaws, neck, shoulders and back, chest, stomach, buttocks and thighs, legs and calf muscles, foot muscles, end by taking a deep breath.

(d) Assertion techniques: broken record, empathic (friendly) assertion, escalating assertion, and fogging. Show videotape of inappropriate/ appropriate versions of the use of assertion techniques.

(f) Reminders: Things we say to ourselves (overt or covert) to guide our behavior or to get us to remember certain things. Show videotape version of inappropriate/appropriate ways of using reminders.

(g) Thinking-ahead procedure: Another type of reminder that utilizes problem solving and self-instruction to estimate future negative consequences for current misbehavior to a conflict situation. Thinking ahead involves the utilization of the following contingency statement: "If I (*misbehavior*) now, then I will (*future negative consequences*)." Show the videotape of inappropriate/appropriate versions of using the thinking-ahead procedure.

(h) Self-evaluation statements: Reminders that are used after a conflict situation to provide immediate feedback on behavior and feelings during a conflict.

(i) Problem solving:
- What is the problem?
- What can I do?
- What will happen if . . .
- What will I do?
- How did it work?

In closing this session it is important to review the rationale for using self-control techniques, placing special emphasis on the fact that responsibility for appropriate behavior and consequences (positive and negative) lies with the individual student and that he/she makes the choices.

This discussion should be followed by thanking the participants for their cooperation and designating the two students who exhibited outstanding cooperation and participation by rewarding them with additional reinforcers.

Chapter 4

Implementing Individual Anger Control Treatment

PRETREATMENT ISSUES

Selecting Target Adolescents

Group Versus Individual Treatment

There are several clinical reasons why individual anger control treatment might be indicated for a particular adolescent. The need for individual treatment may be due to the adolescent not having the necessary motivation, verbal skills, insights into problem areas, or intellectual capabilities to benefit from group treatment. Individual short-term crisis intervention is necessary, if the adolescent's anger control problem is life threatening or dangerous to others (e.g., self-abuse, suicidal gestures, high frequency of destructive or assaultive behavior). Individual therapy is also indicated if the adolescent's capacity for forming relationships is impaired to the extent of extreme social isolation. Additional individual treatment may also be required following group treatment, due to poor skill acquisition or faulty application. Furthermore, adolescents who are physically handicapped (e.g., impaired sight or hearing), or have concerns about confidentiality in a group situation that make them unwilling to self-disclose information, may require individual treatment. Finally, adolescents may just prefer individual over group treatment.

In the outpatient clinic setting, there are practical issues concerning groups versus individual treatment. Recruitment of group members, scheduling sessions, transportation, group noncohesiveness, communication with significant others, and access to situations where problems actually occur may be factors that mitigate against group treatment (Feindler et al., 1984a).

Prior to the presentation of the training program to the adolescent, it is critical for the therapist to consider referral sources in order to determine if individual anger control training is the most appropriate clinical intervention at this time.

This can be accomplished by conducting a thorough behavioral interview with referral sources in the adolescent's immediate environment. If you are a professional working in an inpatient or residential setting, gathering relevant information about the adolescent will be easy due to the close proximity of professionals who work with the adolescent. If you work in an outpatient setting, this information-gathering task will be more difficult in terms of interviewing the adolescent's significant others (e.g., parents, teachers, school psychologists, involved relatives, and siblings). In gathering all relevant information, the therapist should prompt these sources to identify the situational antecedents that provoke the adolescent's anger-aggressive outbursts, the physiological, affective, and behavioral components of the adolescent's anger response, and the resulting consequences. Information concerning the frequency and duration of anger/aggressive outbursts and any attempts at anger control by the adolescent is helpful. Thus, the goal of this evaluation should be to obtain as much information about the adolescent's most recent anger-aggressive patterns from as many sources as possible.

Contracting with Adolescents: How to Present Program Rationale

Conducting the Initial Behavioral Interview with the Adolescent

In the initial interview with the adolescent, the therapist should share the relevant information gathered about recent anger-aggressive outbursts as reported by significant others. The goal here is to educate the adolescent about how others in the immediate environment view his/her anger patterns and to find out what they think are the possible events that trigger such reactions.

Following this sharing of information, the therapist will direct the adolescent through a functional analysis of anger patterns via an ABC format (i.e., antecedent—behavior—consequence). Conflicts are assessed in this fashion because it allows for complex interactions to be broken down into understandable categories. The therapist can ask the adolescent to identify five triggers (A) that without fail lead to loss of anger control and to elaborate on those triggers that provoke the greatest amount of anger and aggression. These triggers should be listed on a blackboard by the therapist.

Next the therapist should instruct the adolescent to talk about how he/she reacts (B) to each of the triggers listed on the blackboard. The behaviors or reactions can be divided into three categories by asking the following questions:

- "What do you *think* about when your anger is triggered?" (cognitive component)
- "What do you *feel* like when your anger is triggered?" (affective-physiological component)
- "What do you *act* like or what do you do when your anger is triggered?" (behavioral component)

Finally the therapist should cue the adolescent to talk about the consequences (C) that immediately follow the anger-aggressive behavior. After listing them on the board, the adolescent can place a plus or minus sign next to each consequence, indicating his/her perception of the consequences as either positive or negative. Following this rating, the therapist should score each consequence as if a scorekeeper of a baseball game. A positive consequence represents a homerun for the adolescent, and a negative consequence represents a homerun for the trigger. Homeruns (points) are tallied up by the therapist. In most cases, if the adolescent's perception of the consequences are accurate, then the trigger usually wins the ballgame. In those cases in which the adolescent identifies positive consequences for aggression and negative consequences for nonaggression, the therapist can do some values-clarification work with the adolescent (Simon, Howe, & Kirschenbaum, 1972).

Next the adolescent's behavior (B) and consequence (C) responses previously listed should be erased. The therapist then will explain to the adolescent that by learning how to use anger control skills effectively, he/she can be the "winner" of positive consequences and actually "shutout or hold the trigger scoreless." The therapist should further make clear that the adolescent may not be able to change the trigger, but his/her reaction to the trigger can be changed so that the outcome will be more positive.

Describing the Anger Control Program to the Adolescent

The next step for the therapist is to get the adolescent further hooked into The Art of Self-Control individual program. The following two paradigm rationales are offered as examples for presentation to adolescents.

1. "The first goal of the program is to increase your personal power during anger provoking situations. By increasing and improving your self _____ ." The therapist will then conduct the self-(fill in the blank) exercise and prompt the adolescent to use the following words in order to define what personal power means. If needed, the therapist can provide the adolescent with the first few letters of each word. Be sure to list words on blackboard.

- self-control
- self-confidence
- self-respect
- self-responsibility

The therapist will then add the following words to the adolescent's list.

- self-integrity
- self-assessment
- self-relaxation
- self-assertion
- self-instructions
- self-problem solving

The therapist should then provide the following brief definitions for each of the above mentioned terms:

- *self-control*—how well and how fast you can control your anger and then how positively you can express it.
- *self-confidence*—the faith you have in your ability to control your anger.
- *self-respect*—being able to rely and depend upon yourself to control your anger now and in the future.
- *self-integrity*—controlling your anger in a way that honestly serves not only your best interests but also others who care about you.
- *self-assessment*—your ability to stop and look at what you need to do to control your anger.
- *self-relaxation*—your ability to stay calm during anger-provoking situations.
- *self-assertion*—your ability to express yourself in a direct, open, honest way during anger-provoking situations.
- *self-instructions*—your ability to instruct yourself quietly to calm down and then to express your anger in a positive manner.
- *self-problem solving*—your ability to choose the most appropriate anger control skills to use in a given anger-provoking situation.

2. "The second goal of this program is to teach you how to stay out of the fool's ring* by cutting the fool's strings." The therapist will then draw a circle on the blackboard, placing an X in the middle of the circle and an X outside of the circle.

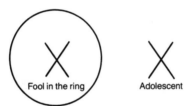

The therapist will then inform the adolescent that the X in the circle represents the fool in the ring (i.e., the anger-provoking trigger), and the X outside of the circle represents the adolescent. The fool has no personal power whatsoever and is in the circle only to pull on the adolescents' strings (i.e., provoke the adolescent's anger).

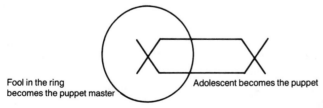

*We are indebted to James Almedina, staff psychologist at Sagamore Children's Center, for his valuable input into the "Fool in the Ring" paradigm.

If the adolescent allows his/her strings to be pulled by the fool in the ring, the fool then becomes the puppetmaster, and the adolescent becomes the puppet. Then there are two fools in the ring.

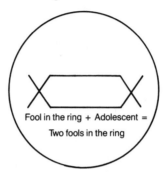

Fool in the ring + Adolescent =
Two fools in the ring

The therapist will explain to the adolescent that by entering the fool's ring he/she is giving up personal power and is thus playing the fool's game rather than his/her own. The second goal of the program is not to give up personal power by entering the fool's ring, but to use anger control skills to cut the fool's strings.

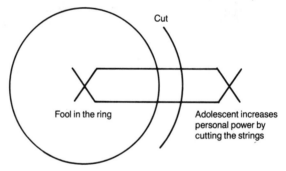

Cut

Fool in the ring

Adolescent increases
personal power by
cutting the strings

Following the presentation of the fool in the ring paradigm, the therapist will then discuss what will be expected of the adolescent during his or her participation in The Art of Self-Control individual anger control program. These expectations are best clarified via a written contract such as the one shown in Table 4.1.

For adolescents residing in an inpatient or residential facility, we recommend that 1-hour sessions be provided three times a week for a 6-week period. In outpatient settings, 90-minute sessions should be provided weekly for a period of 12 weeks. Furthermore, we cannot overemphasize the importance of encouraging adolescents and their significant others to provide ongoing verbal evaluative feedback to the therapist concerning anger control skills application failures or successes. By making this feedback an integral part of the program, the therapist will be enhancing the continuity and effectiveness of the program on a session to session basis.

Table 4.1. Sample Anger Control Training Contract

Consent to Participate in Training Project

Purpose: This project is designed to teach me how to better control my anger when I get into conflictive situations with other people.

1. The training project (cognitive and behavioral approaches to anger control training) has been explained to me thoroughly by Ms. ____ and Mr. ____ .
2. I understand that my participation in this project is completely voluntary and that I may withdraw at any time without consequences.
3. I understand that I will receive daily minute training sessions with Ms. ____ and one of the specialty teachers for about 5 weeks.
4. I understand that these sessions will be videotaped and that I will be able to see my videotapes on request. These videotapes will be used only for this project.
5. I understand that I will be asked to fill out some questionnaires and to participate in some role plays before and after this training project.
6. I understand that my participation in this project will be told to no one unless I give my permission. All of the questionnaires that I fill out will have my name removed so that my responses will be confidential.
7. I am aware that I will be working on controlling my anger during these training sessions, which may sometimes cause me to get upset or angry.
8. I understand that Mr. ____ will be available at all times to answer any questions I might have about this training program.
9. I have read all of the above and I agree to participate in this training program.

Signed: _____

Witness: _____

Project Investigator: _____

Training Methods

Therapist's Preparation for Training Program

The therapist conducting individual treatment should utilize the same teaching techniques and strategies as in group anger control training (discussed in detail in chapter 3) to enhance adolescent skill acquisition and application. Furthermore, the stress inoculation training goals (i.e., prevention, regulation, and execution) and phases (education, acquisition, and application) are implemented in the same manner as in group treatment. Anger control methods (live and symbolic modeling, coaching, behavioral rehearsal, and role-play practice during individual sessions) are presented via lecture and discussion. Structured feedback is provided by the positive and negative stop-gap approach. During each session, the adolescent will be encouraged to present current conflict situations to the therapist via the hassle log and other self-monitoring devices and identify problem behaviors, generate alternatives, and evaluate response consequences on a session to session basis.

SESSION BY SESSION DESCRIPTION
OF THE ART OF SELF-CONTROL
INDIVIDUAL ANGER CONTROL
TRAINING PROGRAM

The following pages provide a detailed session by session description of the individual anger control program that we have used in outpatient settings. This program manual can be easily adapted for inpatient use by extending the content covered in two sessions across three sessions. The content is equivalent to the group program; however, the therapist's presentation style and the amount of time and attention afforded to discussion of conflict situations during one-to-one sessions are different.

Session 1

1. Review the two goals of the training program:

   (a) to increase personal power during anger-provoking situations
   (b) to learn how to stay out of the fool's ring by cutting the fool's strings

2. Review ABC self-assessment training. Remind adolescent that future conflict situations will be discussed using this type of format.

3. Introduce to adolescent how anger really occurs. Sketch the picture of the match and firecracker on the blackboard (adapted from Novaco's cognitive model for Anger Arousal, 1979).

Explain to the adolescent in the following manner: "When the trigger goes off, it ignites two types of reactions at the same time. In your mind you will have certain negative thoughts and feelings about the trigger. You might think what's happening to you is unfair, awful, or terrible. You might feel frustrated, annoyed, threatened, irritated, resentful, or hassled. As a result of these negative reactions occurring in your mind, your body will also react in an out-of-control manner. Inside your body you might experience muscle tightness or tension, butterflies in the stomach, increased heart rate and blood pressure, sweating, or shortening of breath. You might also exhibit the following: nervousness, clenched fists, rigid body posture, angry stares or squinting of the eyes, red face, cold and clammy hands, yelling, cursing, hitting, threatening gestures, and throwing objects. Basically your body and mind will be feeding off each other's reactions. The longer you have negative thoughts and feelings concerning the trigger, the more your body will react in an out-of-control manner. So it is not so much the trigger that makes you angry, but it is actually the way your mind and body react to the trigger that makes you angry. Picture your mind and body as if they were a firecracker. The match that ignites or lights the fuse is the trigger. The fuse is your mind, and your body is the contents of the firecracker. The longer you let the fuse

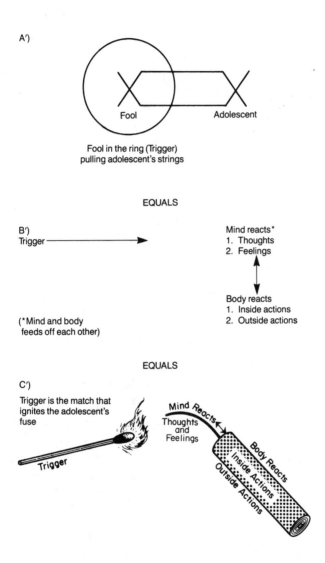

A')

Fool   Adolescent

Fool in the ring (Trigger)
pulling adolescent's strings

EQUALS

B')
Trigger ⟶

Mind reacts*
1. Thoughts
2. Feelings

Body reacts
1. Inside actions
(*Mind and body   2. Outside actions
feeds off each other)

EQUALS

C')
Trigger is the match that
ignites the adolescent's
fuse

Trigger

Mind Reacts
Thoughts
and
Feelings

Body Reacts
Inside Actions
Outside Actions

burn, the more you risk blowing up and losing control of your anger. How quickly you put the fuse out depends upon how well and how quickly you can stop and control your negative thoughts and feelings. Remember the sooner you put the fuse out (i.e., cut the fool's strings) the more personal power you will have over your actions in terms of dealing with the anger-provoking situation effectively."

4. Begin brief relaxation training.

   (a) Introduce deep breathing-cue word technique: Explain to the adolescent that the simplest way to learn how to relax is to breathe deeply and fully. First model how to properly take a deep breath in front of the adolescent, and then prompt the adolescent to behaviorally rehearse the technique. Provide corrective feedback when needed. Provide the following modeling guidelines in teaching this deep breathing technique. "Place one hand on your stomach, breathe in slowly through your nose, feeling your lungs fill completely with air. As you breathe in slowly, your hand should move outward. Once your lungs are completely filled with air, breathe out fully and completely through your mouth. As you breathe out, practice saying the following cue words out loud and then quietly to yourself: chill-out, relax, calm down, slow down, ignore, keep cool. Adding words to your deep breathing will allow you to become further relaxed.

(b) Introduce deep breathing-cue statement technique: Explain to the adolescent that by adding statements such as: "I am calm and relaxed" to deep breathing, he/she will become further relaxed.

Note: In training the adolescent to use the deep breathing cue word and statement techniques the therapist should instruct the adolescent to use his/her physiological tension as a signal to deep breathe. The following rationale for using the deep breathing techniques is provided:

- reduces tension
- shifts attention away from the trigger (i.e., fool in the ring) to mind and body control
- gives time to think about what needs to be done so that anger can be expressed in a positive manner

(c) Introduce additional deep breathing techniques as methods the adolescent can use when needing more time to calm down.

- Deep breathing, backward counting technique. With this technique, verbally instruct the adolescent to do the following: "Take a deep breath and as you breathe out say the number 10 out loud. Take a deep breath and as you breathe out say out loud 9 and then say "I am more relaxed and calm at 9 than I was at 10." Take a deep breath and as you breathe out say 8 and then say "I am more relaxed and calm at 8 than I was at 9." This procedure will continue until the adolescent finishes with the counting of each descending number followed by a statement of being "more relaxed and calm." Prompt the adolescent to first rehearse this technique out loud and then quietly during role-play practice. During this role-play practice, adolescents should be prompted to turn away from the anger-provoking trigger and to count backwards using a slow, measured pace.

- Deep breathing, pleasant thinking technique: Instruct adolescent to use his/her imagination for a moment by closing eyes and describing a pleasant outdoor scene. Therapist should prompt the adolescent to be as descriptive as possible, tuning the adolescent into colors and surroundings. The adolescent's description of the pleasant outdoor scene should ideally be 8 to 10 minutes in duration. The pleasant scene description and review can be used as a coping alternative in dealing with anger-provoking situations.

5. Assign self-monitoring homework: Therapist can choose from the handout options noted in Figures 4.1, 4.2, and 4.3.

FIGURE 4.1. Openended hassle sheet

Name: _____
Date: _____
Morn: _____ Aft. _____ Eve. _____

HASSLE SHEET

Where were you?

What happened? (Who made you angry?)

Who was that somebody?

What were you thinking?

What did you do? (What techniques did you use to control your anger? Or what happened to you as a result of not controlling your anger?)

How did you handle yourself?

1	2	3	4	5
Poorly	Not so well	Okay	Good	Great

How angry were you?

1	2	3	4	5
Burning mad	Really angry	Moderately angry	Mildly angry but still okay	Not angry at all

FIGURE 4.2. ABC worksheet

Name: _____
Date: _____

USING YOUR TECHNIQUES

Which technique did you use?

_____

_____

A _____→ B _____→ C _____
   Trigger   Behavior   Consequence

Authorization (The staff saw it) _____

My Signature _____

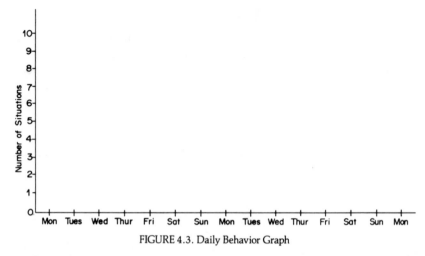

FIGURE 4.3. Daily Behavior Graph

The therapist should use the homework assignments listed in Table 4.2 throughout the training program. The rationale for self-monitoring is that it provides the adolescent an opportunity to give the therapist an accurate picture of how he/she is dealing with anger-provoking situations during the week.

Table 4.2. Homework Assignments for Individual Anger Control Training

---

a. *What Gets You Angry?* is a trigger hierarchy exercise that requires the adolescent to list what triggers his/her anger from most angriest to least angriest.

b. *Open-Ended Hassle Sheets* is an adopted version of the hassle log checklist that requires the adolescent to provide a brief written response to a series of open ended questions (see Figure 4.1).

c. *Angry Behavior Worksheet* is an exercise that requires the adolescent to identify the angry behaviors of others (e.g., teachers) and then to identify his/her own angry behavior. These can be listed on a designated form.

d. *ABC Worksheet* is an exercise that requires the adolescent to use anger control skills in real-life conflicts. The adolescent is required to report in writing what anger control technique was used; what was the trigger in the conflict; and what were the consequences (See Figure 4.2).

e. *Daily Behavior Graph* is an exercise that requires the adolescent to graph the number of conflict situations experienced daily (See Figure 4.3).

Session 2

1. Review completed homework assignments.

2. Review all brief relaxation skills, prompting rehearsal of all skills through spontaneous role-play practice. Remind adolescent of the importance of using his or her tension as a signal to slow down and deep breathe.

3. Continue self-assessment training. Explain the difference between indirect and direct anger-provoking triggers. Prompt adolescent to identify additional cues that signal tension.

4. Introduce active progressive muscle relaxation training of tensing and relaxing systematic muscle groups.

(a) Provide the following rationale: "By physically tensing your muscles and then relaxing them you will be able to recognize the clear difference between feeling tense and feeling relaxed."

(b) Provide the following guidelines: "Sit in a comfortable position. Take off your shoes. Close your eyes. Tense only one muscle group at a time and only to 70–80% of your capacity. If you experience pain while tensing a particular muscle group, stop immediately. Upon tensing, breathe in through your nose, hold tension, and count to 5. Then say to yourself *Relax now,*' breathing out through your mouth, releasing the tension in that muscle group immediately. Wait 15 seconds, paying close attention to the relaxed feeling in that particular muscle group (such as warmth, heaviness, looseness, and tingling sensations in the muscles). Repeat tense-relax cycle for that particular muscle group again."

(c) Provide adolescent with training in taking basic physiological self-ratings such as pulse rate, hand temperature (using finger thermometer), and subjective ratings of tension/relaxation level using a numerical scale from 1–10 (1 = very relaxed; 10 = very tense). Therapist should prompt adolescent to take physiological ratings before and after relaxation practice.

(d) Model progressive muscle relaxation exercise and pre- and posttaking of physiological ratings. The following order of tensing and relaxing muscle groups is strongly recommended. Jacobsen's original relaxation exercises have been adapted for use with an adolescent population. Table 4.3 presents this abbreviated version. Each muscle group should be tensed and relaxed twice.

Table 4.3. Abbreviated Sequence for Muscle Relaxation

	Major muscle group
1. Clench both fists	hands and forearms
2. Bend both elbows	biceps
3. Frown, squint eyes, clench teeth	face, eyes, jaw
4. Push head back and forth	neck
5. Shrug and rotate shoulders	shoulders, upper chest
6. Tense stomach muscles as if you were preparing for a blow to the stomach	abdominal and buttock region
7. Raise both legs straight out, curling feet upward	thighs
8. Push both legs down into the floor, curling toes downward	knees, calves, feet and toes

(e) Prompt the adolescent to behaviorally rehearse the progressive muscle relaxation exercise. We recommend that the adolescent be videotaped doing this exercise so that corrective feedback using the stop-gap method can be provided following completion of the exercise. Make sure you prompt the adolescent to take physiological and subjective ratings before and after this exercise.

5. Assign self-monitoring homework: daily behavior graphs, ABC worksheets, and/or hassle logs. Instruct the adolescent to do daily active progressive muscle relaxation practice during the next week and to report in writing on hassle log or ABC worksheet physiological and subjective ratings before and after daily practice. The rationale in doing daily relaxation practice is to help the adolescent gradually achieve a conditioned relaxation response to his/her tension cues. After several practice sessions (15–20), the adolescent will be able to calm down when faced with an anger-provoking situation by becoming aware of the muscles that are tense and then relaxing them.

Session 3

1. Review completed homework assignments.
2. Review all brief relaxation skills.
3. Review active progressive muscle relaxation training. Prompt adolescent to rehearse the exercise with you. Check to make sure proper procedure is being used in terms of order, timing of tense-relax cycle, deep breathing, and "relax now" cuing.
4. Introduce passive progressive muscle relaxation training (Mason, 1980), which does not involve tensing of muscles. This exercise also incorporates the adolescent's use of deep breathing, backward counting, and imagery techniques. Before conducting this exercise, the adolescent should take physiological and subjective ratings of tension/relaxation level. This exercise requires active concentration in terms of listening to the suggestions provided by the therapist during the script reading. Encourage the adolescent to let the suggestions and/or words do the work. Prompt the adolescent to get into a comfortable sitting position, close eyes, and get ready to listen. Then read the script in Table 4.4 in a calm, slowly paced voice. This script can also be taperecorded and played during homework practice.

Following the exercise in Table 4.4, prompt the adolescent to take physiological and subjective ratings of tension/relaxation level. Review with the adolescent any difficulty that was experienced while visualizing the waves, elevator ride, or the outdoor scene. Was the overall exercise pleasant and relaxing? Suggest that when he/she is faced with an anger-provoking situation, this type of relaxation skill might be helpful.

5. Assign self-monitoring homework: daily behavior graphs, ABC worksheets, and/or hassle logs. Also continue to prompt the adolescent to practice active progressive muscle relaxation on a daily basis; to begin using brief relaxation skills more frequently in daily conflicts; and provide the adolescent with a tape of passive relaxation training to listen to during the next week.

Table 4.4. Passive Muscle Relaxation Script

"Try to get as comfortable as possible. Just breathe in through your nose and breathe out through your mouth fully and completely. With each out breath, quietly allow all the tensions to leave your body. Just breathe in slowly, naturally, and deeply, and breathe out freely and completely. You have the power and the will to let your daily thoughts and concerns drift out of your mind. Imagine you are watching ocean waves coming in and going out, coming in and going out. The waves going out are your thoughts leaving you and the waves coming in are waves of relaxation spreading throughout your body. As your mind calms and clears completely, all thoughts and distractions will leave you just by breathing them away.

Picture yourself on the tenth floor of a modern skyscraper. You are about to enter onto a very slow moving elevator. Hold onto the side rail so that you feel safe as you slowly drift down from floor to floor. As the floors pass by you, you will become more deeply relaxed. Imagine you have just passed the ninth floor and are slowly drifting down to the eighth floor. As you drift down to this floor, pay attention to relaxing your arms and hands. Just let these muscles go completely loose and limp. Let your arms and hands sink into the surface they are resting on, becoming further relaxed and very heavy. If you are feeling any tension in your arms or hands, just breathe it away as you slowly pass by the eighth floor and gradually drift to the seventh floor into a much deeper relaxation. As you approach the seventh floor, continue to breathe in deeply and breathe out fully and completely. As you continue your downward descent on this very slow moving elevator pay attention to your forehead and let it relax by becoming calm and smooth. Let the muscles around your eyes become relaxed by just breathing calmly and naturally. Allow this relaxed feeling to spread down around your jaw and into your mouth as the slow moving elevator passes the seventh floor. Pay attention to the muscles in your neck as you drift into a deeper relaxation, and if you are feeling any tightness in this area just let it go by breathing it away. Relax your shoulders as the elevator you are riding on slowly drifts down to the sixth floor. Let this very deep relaxation spread to your chest and stomach area as you slowly pass by the sixth floor. Notice now how you are in a much calmer relaxed state than you were when you entered onto the elevator on the 10th floor. Relax your back now as your drift slowly by the fifth floor, becoming much more relaxed and at ease. Allow this relaxation to deepen as you breathe more naturally and calmly. Pay attention to the upper parts of your legs and notice how this area of your body is becoming comfortably heavy and warm. You are now approaching the fourth floor as your upper legs sink into the cushions they are resting on. As you pass by the fourth floor you are feeling a very deep relaxation, heaviness, and warmth throughout your body. This relaxation and pleasant, comfortable sensation is now spreading further down into your knees as you approach the third floor on this very slow moving elevator. Continue to breathe deeply and naturally as this very deep, heavy relaxation spreads down from your knees into your calves as you drift by the third floor. You are slowly coming to the end of your elevator ride as your legs become heavier and heavier. As you pass by the second floor you can feel the relaxation spreading down into your feet and into your toes. You have now reached the bottom floor. As you get off the elevator you find yourself surrounded by your favorite outdoor scene. This is a favorite place of yours, and you are there by yourself during a very calm and peaceful day. The sky above you is blue, and the grass around you is green. Take a moment and find a comfortable place to lie down in the fresh green grass so that you can feel the warmth of the sun and the coolness of the ever so calm spring breeze. Enjoy the beauty of the very blue sky and listen to the pleasant, natural sounds of the breeze blowing through the leaves of the hills that surround you. You feel very safe and secure in this very private special place. You may go there anytime that you wish just by using your creative imagination and by breathing calmly and naturally. Remember you have control over your tension just by breathing it away and you have the personal power to stay calm by letting your mind have control over your body. When you are ready you may gradually become awake by bringing yourself back into this room. Tell yourself: I am refreshed and awake. Take a deep slow breath now and stretch. And let the feelings of relaxation and calmness you have just experienced stay with you throughout the rest of your day and week."

Session 4

1. Review completed homework assignments.

2. Review all brief relaxation skills and determine how frequently the adolescent is using skills based on self-reports, homework, and reports by significant others.

3. Review active progressive muscle relaxation training. Provide adolescent with high intensity social reinforcement for daily practice and perhaps plan to back up social reinforcement with a spontaneous activity reinforcer (i.e., treat him/her to dinner outside of the facility).

4. Review passive progressive muscle relaxation. Probe to determine if adolescent has been listening to tape during the past week.

5. Introduce autogenic relaxation training (Schultz & Luthe, 1959).

   (a) Provide the following rationale: "Autogenics is quite similar to the last relaxation training we did. It combines deep breathing with statements and/or suggestions that you repeat quietly to yourself during an anger-provoking situation so that you can reduce the amount of tension you are experiencing. It also will allow you to shift your attention away from the anger-provoking trigger to mind and body control. Finally and most importantly it will provide you with more time to think about how you want to express your anger."

   (b) Model the following autogenic procedure out loud: "We will use two adjectives (heavy and warm) in a repetitive manner in order to get certain parts of our body to relax when we are experiencing tension in these areas. When you feel tension in your hands, arms, shoulders, neck, or legs, find a comfortable chair to sit down in. Close your eyes and say the following suggestions or statements to yourself at least three times. In between each set of statements use your deep breathing technique." The therapist will then take a deep breath and say out loud in a calm slow-paced voice:
   - "My hands and arms are heavy and warm." (Three times) (Deep Breath)
   - "My neck and shoulders are heavy and warm." (Three times) (Deep Breath)
   - "My legs and feet are heavy and warm." (Three times) (Deep Breath)

   (c) Prompt the adolescent to take physiological and subjective ratings of tension/relaxation level. Have the adolescent rehearse the technique overtly and then covertly. This should be followed by taking of physiological and subjective ratings of tension/relaxation level.

6. The rest of session 4 should be used to role play all relaxation skills using videotaping equipment and the stop-gap method to provide the adolescent with corrective feedback when needed.

7. Assign self-monitoring homework: daily behavior graphs, ABC worksheets, and/or hassle log. Encourage the adolescent to use all relaxation skills in dealing with daily anger-provoking situations. Provide adolescent with autogenics relaxation tape (optional) if needed.

Sessions 5 and 6

The next two individual sessions are similar to the assertion training group sessions discussed in the previous chapter. Therefore, the therapist is encouraged to refer back to sessions 4 and 5 and follow the same format recommended in the group anger control training manual.

Session 7

1. Review completed homework assignments.
2. Review all relaxation skills.
3. Review the four assertion techniques taught so far.
4. Introduce additional assertion techniques to be implemented by the adolescent when feeling manipulated by others.

(a) I Language assertion (Lange & Jakubowski, 1976): Explain to the adolescent that this technique can be used to assert or express difficult negative feelings. Provide the following script and model its proper use out loud: "When you (describe the other person's behavior), I feel or the effects are (describe the consequences). I would prefer (describe the behavior change)". In addition, model the I Language technique one step further by clarifying the consequences that will result from the other person's behavior change.

(b) How to say "no" effectively (Fensterheim & Ball, 1975): Explain to the adolescent that there are negative consequences that occur when you want to say no but can't. Allowing others to manipulate you continually because of your inability to say no could lead to a possible anger build-up and outburst. Provide the following guidelines for saying no effectively: "When you want to definitely say no, be firm, clear, specific, and honest. Your answer should be short, to the point, and most importantly, start with the word *no*. Try not to be overly apologetic. When necessary, provide the other person another course of action." The therapist should then model this technique.

5. The rest of the session should be spent rehearsing and role playing with techniques using videotape equipment and the stop-gap method when corrective feedback is needed.

6. Assign self-monitoring homework: daily behavior graphs, ABC worksheet, and/or hassle log. The therapist should also encourage the adolescent to use both relaxation and assertion skills in dealing with daily anger-provoking situations.

Sessions 8, 9, and 10

The next three individual sessions are similar to the self-instruction training group sessions discussed in the previous chapter. Therefore, the therapist is encouraged to refer back to sessions 6 through 10 in chapter 3 and to follow the same format recommended in the group anger control training manual. In addition, we also recommend that in these three individual sessions the therapist provide the following self-instructional training to the adolescent.

1. *Cognitive restructuring* (Ellis, 1977): In session 1 of this individual anger control training, we discussed in great detail how anger occurs and concluded that the mind (beliefs, attitudes, and feelings) has tremendous influence over behavior. Through a simplified diagram the adolescents are shown how their negative thoughts can cause them to lose control of their anger. Before providing the adolescent with reminders training, we recommend that the therapist do the following cognitive restructuring training procedure.

(a) The therapist should explain to the adolescent the following rationale for using a self-assessment approach in restructuring his/her faulty appraisals or negative self-statements. "Like a carpenter who is hired to make repairs or rebuild something, we too, when we find something faulty or weak with the way we think about the trigger, must restructure or rebuild that thought into something more positive. When our thoughts are of an extreme, negative nature we must in some way learn how to tone them down by moderating their intensity. If we don't, these intense negative thoughts or self-statements will lead to our loss of personal power, causing us to enter into the fool's ring. By doing a self-assessment of our intense or faulty negative thoughts we will have the opportunity to rebuild and restructure these thoughts into something more positive.

(b) The therapist should then present the steps of self-assessments (see Table 4.5) and model how to use them.

2. *Thought Stopping* (Wolpe, 1973):

(a) Explain to the adolescent that thought stopping is a procedure that can interrupt his/her negative thoughts abruptly.

(b) Have the adolescent close his/her eyes in order to demonstrate the power of this technique. Prompt the adolescent to think about something really negative or disturbing. After a few minutes the therapist will then shout loudly, "Stop!" If the adolescent reports that his/her negative thought has ceased, then the therapist should further instruct the adolescent that some positive thoughts or activity should now be substituted in place of the negative thought (for example, relaxation, assertion, or self-instructions).

This skill training will be an excellent lead-in to reminders training.

Table 4.5. Self-Assessment Steps for Anger Control

1. Identify the tension.
2. Identify what triggered the tension.
3. Identify the negative thought connected to the tension.
4. Challenge or dispute the negative thought.
5. Tone down or rebuild the thought or substitute positive thought in place of negative one.

3. *Self-instruction training* (i.e., reminders): Occasionally, the therapist will work with an adolescent who will need a simplified version of the reminders terminology. Table 4.6 presents types and definitions of self-guiding speech.

Session 11

1. Review completed homework assignments, relaxation skills and rationale, assertion skills and rationale, self-instruction skills and rationale.

2. Introduce the Angry Behavior Cycle concept. This training will focus on the self-modification of overt aggressive responses of the adolescent which may provoke others (including friends, family, and other adults) into conflict situations. Teaching the adolescent to identify the responses of others to his/her anger expression and aggressive behavior, and to understand the interactive sequence that prompts the escalation of conflict situations, will extend his/her self-control. The modification of aggressive behavior early in the sequence will serve to preempt an escalation.

(a) Describe the various responses that others may have when they observe the adolescent's overt anger cues. Include the following responses: "They may ignore you, laugh at you, tell you to shut up or lay off. They may tell the teacher or engage in a variety of aggressive behaviors to defend themselves or to further provoke you." Be sure to tie these descriptions in with concrete situations the adolescent reported in his/her hassle logs.

Table 4.6. Typology of Self-Statements

1. *Quiet reminders* (covert) are those self-statements you say quietly to yourself before and during conflicts to guide and direct your behavior in a self-controlled manner.
2. *Loud (overt) reminders* are instructions or statements you give to others out loud to help guide and direct their behavior before and during conflicts in a self-controlled manner.
3. *Quiet (covert) thinking-ahead reminders* are anticipated negative consequences that you can use quietly on yourself as reminders not to get involved in future negative behavior.
4. *Loud (overt) thinking-ahead reminders* are anticipated negative consequences that you can use out loud on others as reminders for them not to get involved in future negative behavior.
5. *Quiet after-reminders* for resolved conflicts are those quiet reminders you can use to reward yourself for a job well done. Do not dwell on unresolved conflicts, and use the thinking-ahead procedure to decide what you have to do to handle the conflict better the next time.
6. *Loud after-reminders* for resolved conflicts are those loud reminders you say to others to reward them for a job well done. For unresolved conflicts, use loud reminders on others and then remind them to use the thinking-ahead procedure to think about how they will handle the conflict better the next time.

(b) Ask the adolescent to describe what his/her reactions would be after the other persons involved are provoked. Prompt the adolescent to identify some escalating behaviors, increases in frequency and/or intensity of aggressive behavior (e.g., yelling louder and louder, cursing more and more, hitting, throwing objects, threatening, etc).

(c) Describe the cyclical components of these interactive sequences and the probable negative consequences due to the escalation of the conflict utilizing the following ABC format:

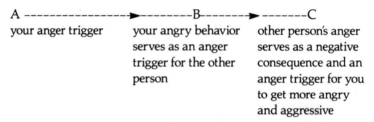

A ---------------▶--------B-------▶-------C
your anger trigger   your angry behavior   other person's anger
                        serves as an anger   serves as a negative
                        trigger for the other consequence and an
                        person   anger trigger for you
                                              to get more angry
                                              and aggressive

(d) Also point out to the adolescent that escalated conflicts have ongoing ABCs for both people involved unless the conflict is interrupted early in the cyclical chain. Draw the ABC cyclical chain on the blackboard as follows:

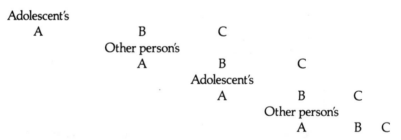

Adolescent's
    A   B   C
             Other person's
                 A   B   C
                         Adolescent's
                             A   B   C
                                     Other person's
                                         A   B   C

Emphasize the importance of using anger control skills to interrupt and stop potential anger conflicts right at the beginning of the chain.

(e) Conduct several role plays with the adolescent prompting use of anger control skills (i.e., relaxation, assertion, reminders) as the only sensible ways to react to the first anger trigger.

3. Assign self-monitoring homework: daily behavior graphs, ABC worksheets, and/or hassle logs. Encourage the adolescent to use all anger control skills in dealing with daily conflicts during the next week.

Session 12

1. Review completed homework assignments.
2. Review all anger control skills and rationales.

3. Provide adolescent with a set of cue (index) cards that list each anger control skill and rationale for use.

4. Conduct problem-solving training. (Refer back to chapter 3 for a detailed description of the five problem-solving stages.)

    (a) Present the following problem-solving sequence on a blackboard:
        What is the problem ———►Identify trigger (A)
        What can I do ———►Brainstorm possible reactions (B)
        What will happen if ———►List consequences to all reactions (C)
        What will I do ———►Pick the best choices
        How did it work ———►Use afterreminders

    b) Using a symbolic modeling videotape or live role play, prompt the adolescent to use above problem-solving sequence and cue index cards in solving the various conflicts.

    (c) Present several hypothetical conflict situations the adolescent might face in the future and again prompt him/her to use problem-solving sequence and cue index cards to solve the hypothetical conflicts.

    (d) Conduct several spontaneous role plays with the adolescent using videotape equipment and stop-gap feedback method in the following manner:
    Therapist will barb adolescent—

- Stop action
- Ask adolescent to quickly identify trigger and four anger control skills he/she could use in response to the trigger
- Start action
- Playback role play and reinforce adolescent for effective selection and use of anger control skills.
- Repeat with different role-play scenario

5. Review all anger control skills and rationales again with adolescent without use of cue index cards.

6. Schedule future booster session.

7. Take adolescent out to celebrate his/her successful completion of individual anger control training program.

Working with Other Family Members

There will be occasions in which it is either necessary or advantageous to work with members of the adolescent's family in terms of individual anger control treatment. Through ongoing analysis of the conflicts that the adolescent presents in individual sessions, the therapist can determine if other family members are contributing to the anger control problems. In fact, many referrals are a result of both the adolescent and other family members losing control of their anger in a cyclical pattern (i.e., Angry Behavior Cycle). If it is evident that other family members are experiencing anger control problems, they should also receive treatment. Other family members might not require intensive anger control treatment, but might only need training in one or two of the skill component areas (e.g., relaxation and assertion). Furthermore, as with any treatment program, it is essential that significant others be periodically informed about what the adolescent has learned in terms of anger control so they can reinforce the adolescent whenever they observe him/her using anger control skills.

CASE STUDIES OF INDIVIDUAL ANGER CONTROL TRAINING

The Case of Eddie

Eddie was a 16-year-old adolescent who was hospitalized for explosive, violent behavior exhibited at home. His clinical diagnosis at admission was Intermittent Explosive Disorder, and his intellectual functioning was in the mild borderline range of mental retardation. Prior to individual anger control treatment, Eddie had been residing in the hospital for 11 months. During this period of time he averaged three aggressive outbursts per week in which he either became physically aggressive toward direct care staff or other patients, self-abusive (banging his head and hands), or violently destructive of property. On most occasions when Eddie lost control he would require mechanical restraint (straight jacket or full sheet restraints) and stat medication.

Our first encounter with Eddie was when he attended an anger control group session. During the first 5 minutes of this particular session, Eddie had a seemingly unprovoked explosive outburst. He physically attacked a direct care staff member, was removed from the group room, placed into mechanical restraint, and given stat medication. Following this episode, Eddie refused to attend future group anger control sessions occurring on his living unit. Due to Eddie's continuous aggressive outbursts during the next few months, which created a great deal of tension among direct care staff and other patients, he was transferred to another living unit.

Our next encounter with Eddie was during a weekend in which we were collecting restriction data from his living unit for program evaluation purposes. On this particular occasion, Eddie experienced another explosive outburst in which he began violently kicking the living unit's entrance door. Instead of letting Eddie continue with this destructive outburst, we opened the entrance door and walked with him to the front of the hospital where we sat for a few minutes. At that time, with a very recent example of temper loss, we offered Eddie an individual treatment program.

Eddie participated actively in 15 individual anger control training sessions. While learning to identify antecedent triggers, he became particularly skilled in using brief relaxation and self-instruction techniques. During his participation in individual treatment, Eddie's explosive outbursts were reduced from an average of 12 outbursts per month (pretreatment) to 2.3 outbursts per month, and there were no incidents requiring mechanical restraints. In addition, because of increased self-control abilities, he was given the opportunity to attend school outside of the hospital. The highpoint of Eddie's progress was exemplified during a group training session that occurred subsequently on his living unit. In this particular group session we had set up an unplanned barb in which one of the co-leaders would enter the group session late, causing the other group leader to have an anger outburst. When the barb occurred, to the pleasant surprise of all, Eddie took the lead and used several loud reminders to calm the angry group leader down.

Eddie was discharged from the hospital 1 month after completing individual anger control training and is now residing in an open residential school setting.

The Case of Wendy

Wendy was a 13-year-old adolescent who was hospitalized due to the physically assaultive and verbal threatening behavior that she was displaying while residing in an open cottage residential program. Prior to this placement she had been residing in a foster care home. Her clinical diagnosis at admission was Conduct Disorder, Undersocialized Aggressive, and her intellectual functioning was in the high average range. Prior to individual anger control treatment, Wendy had been on the short-term crisis unit for a 2-week period. There she was very quick in becoming assaultive with little provocation and destroying property. Wendy had ten isolated explosive outbursts during her first 2 weeks of hospitalization. To complicate matters even more, it was uncertain whether Wendy would be accepted back into her previous placement (a place that she wanted to return to) following her hospitalization. After her second week in the hospital, Wendy was referred by her primary therapist for individual anger control treatment.

Wendy participated in 12 individual anger control training sessions during a 2-week period. The identification of both external triggers and physiological build-up prior to explosive outbursts was quickly understood. She became particularly skilled in brief relaxation, assertion, and problem-solving techniques. During her individual treatment, Wendy's explosive and assaultive outbursts were reduced from an average of five outbursts per week (pretreatment) to one outburst per week (only verbal in nature). The day after Wendy completed her individual training in anger control, she was discharged back to her previous open cottage residential setting. Furthermore, the anger control skills that Wendy was taught were also reviewed with the staff who would be working with her in the cottage program to enhance skill generalization across settings.

Chapter 5

Successful and Unsuccessful Outcomes

ASSURING SUCCESSFUL OUTCOMES

Planning for Maintenance and Generalization

Prompting the Use of Self-Control Techniques

The now classic article by Stokes and Baer (1977) indicated that most developers of behavioral interventions did not, unfortunately, think ahead about planning for the transfer and maintenance of behavior change across settings and time. Most programs seemed geared to the "train and hope" method, which has not proven very reliable. Since that time, however, there have been numerous generalization techniques incorporated into behavioral training programs, and excellent results have been achieved (Kettlewell & Dausch, 1983). If these issues are analyzed prior to the start of any treatment and specific generalization strategies are incorporated, the probability of long-term maintenance of treatment gains is greatly increased.

Varied Training Tasks. A key concept in any skill training program that incorporates behavior rehearsal is *stimulus generalization*. A way to ensure that the anger control skills trained in the program will generalize to various other stimulus situations is to plan numerous role plays of situations relevant to the adolescent. This allows the adolescent to practice the anger management skills in conflict situations that approximate real-life settings. Depending on the population, these situations might include those listed in Table 5.1.

Another method used to ensure generalization of anger control skills would be to conduct some of the sessions in other environments. Although this might initially seem impractical, group meetings complete with role plays can easily be transported to the recreation field, the classroom after school, and the home setting.

Table 5.1. Generalization Scenes

Peer conflict over property, money, relationships, trust, teasing, drugs, sex, and pressure to conform. Family conflict over curfew, household responsibilities, money, friends, personal property, other restrictions, personal hygiene and habits.

Conflict with authority figures such as teachers, counselors, probation officers, policemen, busdrivers, lifeguards, and salespeople. These conflicts usually revolve around rule violation and punishment.

Conflict with unknown peers, other members of groups (those in class, a gang, a ward, etc.) whom the adolescent does not know. These conflicts usually involve some sort of provoking act such as stealing, teasing, and ignoring.

Content of the Cognitive Skills. There have been several investigations comparing the use of different types of self-statements used to control impulsive responding in children. These studies (Kendall, 1981; Schlesser, Meyers, & Cohen, 1981; Thackwray, Meyers, Schlesser, & Cohen, 1985) indicate that those children receiving training with generalized or conceptual self-statements showed better maintenance of self-control across time. They also showed increased generalization to other tasks. It seems that more specific types of self-statements, namely those that are only applicable to the training tasks at hand, do not facilitate the spontaneous application of the techniques to new situations.

Schlesser et al. (1981) suggested that conceptual strategies required the child to be more involved cognitively during the training and subsequent application. Indeed, the child must abstract task information from general self-instructions and adapt the self-control strategy to the new situation at hand. Although these comparative investigations have primarily been conducted using cognitive problem-solving tasks, we can extend the conclusions of these authors to the anger control program. Clearly, given the many variations possible in each type of interpersonal conflict situation, general or conceptual self-statements would be the most effective. Table 5.2 presents a comparison of specific versus general self-statements relevant to an anger provocation scene involving peer threats.

The conceptual self-instructions focus more on the adolescent's own experience during the conflict—on what he/she is feeling and thinking, and what his/her options are in terms of responding to the provocation. The more specific self-instructions focus on the details of the provocation incident in question and are more externally oriented. Sometimes, this focus on the "other guy" may exacerbate the anger already experienced by the adolescent. We suggest teaching the more specific statements at the beginning of the anger control training program and gradually introducing the more advanced conceptual statements toward the end. This will facilitate the other transfer and maintenance strategies employed. Finally, if the adolescents receiving training are cognitively impaired so that there are clear auditory memory or sequencing deficits, then the more general statements may be difficult to decode in the appropriate situation. These adolescents will benefit from more specific strategies.

Table 5.2. Specific Versus General Self-Instructions

Specific:

"This guy is threatening me again. What should I say to him?"

"I have to remember that I can ignore threats. I've done it before, and he usually walks away."

"I'm going to keep my cool and let this guy get in trouble."

"I don't have to even look at him. I'll just walk away and not let it get to me."

"He's the one with the problem. I can handle myself when I get empty threats."

"There's no way he'll follow through, so I'll just ignore."

General:

"I feel some anger. What's getting to me?"

"What's the problem? I need to control my temper."

"I need a plan for dealing with this. I have choices about how to behave. I can handle this. I'll just take my time and think before I act."

"Chill-out. I ain't gonna get all riled up."

"I'll just concentrate on me and what I'm gonna do."

"Hey! I'm handling this fine. No problem."

"What should I do? Walk away and ignore? Deep breath? Tell someone? Assert myself? I'll try one thing. If it doesn't work, I'll try something else."

"I'm in control of my own anger. Terrific!"

Cuing Strategies. Toward the end of the anger control training program and certainly following termination of the program, generalization of self-control skills can be assured if the environment provides some prompts. We have used a variety of both visual and verbal prompts to assist the adolescents in implementing the appropriate techniques.

Preparation for Nonreinforcement or Punishment Contingencies

One of the hoped-for outcomes of any behavior change intervention is that naturally occurring reinforcement contingencies will take over after the formal training is terminated and that the newly acquired skills will be maintained in other environments. Unfortunately this cannot be guaranteed. In actuality, many of the new skills that the adolescent has learned to control his/her anger arousal and to solve interpersonal conflict more effectively will not readily be reinforced. Given the peer/family culture in which the adolescent operates, there may actually be an increase in punishers contingent upon the performance of new and different behaviors. A family system in which verbal aggression is a functional interaction strategy will not naturally provide reinforcements to the adolescent who has learned to walk away and calm down by withdrawing momentarily. Further, family members or other adults who have contact with the adolescent (counselors, teachers, or direct-care staff) usually do not appreciate assertive behavior from adolescents. The anger control program suggests the use of reasonable assertion in order to express opinions and make requests. However, these "rights" are not always afforded to adolescents, who, due to their behavior problems, live in restrictive environments. There are several strategies that, when incorporated into the anger control program, may help the adolescent cope with this lack of reinforcement for new skills.

Coping With Errors. Kendall and Braswell (1985) suggest that part of termination readiness should include skills and cognitive interpretations for overcoming relapse and failure experiences. The adolescent must be prepared to cope with his/her occasional inability to control anger and with failed attempts to implement the skills. Failure experiences can be targeted throughout the training by attending to errors and by guiding the adolescent in the generation of self-statements to use when coping with errors. The adolescent should have some practice in making appropriate attributions and helpful statements when he/she fails (Kendall & Braswell, 1985).

Undoubtedly, adolescents and trainers completing role plays of conflict situations will make mistakes. (If not, we suggest that the trainers purposely plan to make some mistakes so the correction statements can be learned.) Adolescents, following positive evaluations of their role-play performance or the hassles noted in their logs, should be encouraged to point out room for improvement in regard to errors. Should the same scene occur again, optional behaviors should be enumerated, and specific coping statements should be modeled. Table 5.3 presents some examples of statements that adolescents have used when experiencing failure of their anger control skills.

Role Play Potential Conflicts. Another important failure prevention strategy involves the structuring of role plays with persons who may punish the adolescent's newly acquired skills. Trainers, other group members, or actual family members, counselors, or teachers can be involved in these role plays. The antagonist should attempt to punish the use of the adolescent's anger control strategy and continue to provoke and tease the adolescent for not rising to the occasion to fight. The antagonist should also use verbal threats of negative consequences that will

Table 5.3. Coping Statements to Use for Errors

"Uh-oh, made a mistake. Next time I'll think ahead."

"Some of this control stuff is tough, but I'll keep practicing.

"This is new for me. Everyone makes mistakes."

"This stuff won't solve everything, but at least it'll help me keep calmer."

"I gotta remember that I used to really 'lose it,' but now I'm much better controlled."

"It's okay to feel really angry; I just have to concentrate on not letting it take over."

"Some situations are just gonna be harder than others."

occur if the target adolescent continues to stay in control. Once the adolescent has been desensitized to these potential scenarios and has learned both covert and overt methods of handling such a conflict, relapse may be preempted.

Establish Self-Reinforcement Contingencies. The use of positive self-evaluative and self-reinforcement statements should be emphasized in order to prepare for the possible nonreinforcement that may confront the adolescent in the natural environment. The adolescent should be able to positively evaluate either a failed attempt to control his/her anger or continued antagonistic responses from others. The adolescent should be able to pick out the appropriate attributions for the emotional arousal and to outline alternate ways of responding. Again, these strategies should be practiced in the role-play format.

In addition, Bornstein, Hamilton, and McFall (1981) emphasize the modification of negative expectations and self-statements about behaving in an assertive rather than an aggressive manner. More appropriate expectations can be developed through role plays.

Techniques that Facilitate Generalization of Behavior Change

Self-Observation, Self-Monitoring and Self-Reinforcement. Many of the techniques included in the anger control training program are geared toward the self-management of emotional arousal and subsequent responding. These skills, once incorporated into the adolescent's repertoire, are easily transferable to situations other than the training environment. Karoly (1983) defines self-control as a set of cognitive and instrumental processes through which the individual consciously and consistently contributes to changing the likelihood of engaging in a behavior. The implementation of these skills requires the ability to discriminate among rules for standards of behavior in various social situations. It also requires a selective awareness of personal responsibility and the consequences of responses and a commitment to exercise self-control (Karoly, 1983). This motivation, a key factor throughout the anger control program, is influenced by immediate situational factors, generalized expectancies, and a willingness to make an effort toward behavior change. Thus, if the adolescent knows *why* to exercise self-control, *wants to*, and knows *how* to do so (via the skills contained in the program), the chances are that generalization of anger management is enhanced. Indeed, Stokes and Baer (1977) suggested that the mediated controlling responses inherent in self-control interventions would be an appropriate solution to the typically short-term effects of behavioral interventions.

Group Training Sessions. Although, as mentioned, running a group training program with adolescents can be both challenging and taxing, the group format will facilitate the transfer and maintenance of anger control skills. Whether running a residential group in which the adolescents know each other and have established relationships (and conflicts) or an outpatient group, this format provides a closer approximation to the peer contingencies that operate on the adolescent's behavior in most other settings. The role plays conducted with realistic models provide an *in vivo* opportunity for the adolescent to practice newly acquired skills. Further, it is highly probable, given the group dynamics and the rapid rate of adolescent changes, that there will be "real" conflicts within the group. In this case, the adolescents involved may be coached immediately in the appropriate handling of the conflict.

In Vivo Homework Assignment. Another method frequently used in behavior therapy interventions is well-defined homework assignments designed to elicit the performance of newly acquired skills in naturalistic settings. Each session of the anger control program includes assignments of particular skills. If an adolescent seems to have conflicts with a particular person or situational demand, additional homework can be given to prompt further practice. Rather than general instructions ("Try the reminders in five situations this week"), the assignment should be individualized and task-specific ("When your mother starts to nag you about the friends you hang around with and about your not keeping to your curfew, remind yourself not to get upset about it. Use your reminders to stay calm, and then coach yourself to explain calmly where you were and with whom."). Assignments should target all situations facing the adolescent and they can generate their own homework assignments.

Follow-Up Support and Booster Sessions. Termination of training should not be abrupt nor without a plan for individual follow-up of the adolescents. It may be helpful to schedule individual follow-up sessions or alternate ways for the adolescent to get some feedback concerning a particular incident. We have found it helpful for graduates of the program to be invited to talk to new groups about their experiences (thus reinforcing what they have learned) and to their trainers privately when having an anger control problem. This type of open-ended support will help the adolescent to troubleshoot what might have gone awry and what options he/she may have next time. It will also prevent the premature abandonment of self-control skills.

Further, it is advisable to schedule a number of booster sessions following the formal termination of training. Biweekly or monthly discussion sessions will help to further reinforce the adolescents' successes and will promote the maintenance of skills learned and implemented.

Including Significant Others in the Training. Just as the group format provides closer approximations to real-life peer conflicts, the inclusion of significant adults in the training can enhance the generalization of anger control to situations involving authority conflicts. In residential groups, we have often invited the direct care staff to participate in the training. This allows for the *in vivo* role play of any staff-adolescent conflict that may exist; as a side effect, it allows staff members to learn the methodology themselves. They are thus better equipped to reinforce the adolescent's use of a particular technique and may be able to learn to manage their own anger arousal as well.

In an outpatient setting, it may be impractical to invite teachers or probation officers to participate in the training sessions (not to mention that the adolescent might strongly object). However, parents and siblings might be included in some family anger control training sessions. This would require that the therapist coach all members in discrete anger control skills and conduct *very* realistic role plays of family issues. Again, this would enhance transfer and maintenance of the target adolescent's skills.

Further, Bornstein et al. (1981) suggest training significant others in the skills necessary to reward nonaggressive behavior and decrease their own provoking stimulus value.

Systematic Barbs. The barb assessment technique described in chapter 2 can be incorporated in all phases of treatment and is especially helpful in obtaining transfer. This technique, which involves the planned and unplanned provocation of the adolescent in environments other than the training setting, may be more practical in a residential setting. However, if cooperation from significant others has been obtained, they too can be taught how to deliver barbs and how to provide the adolescent with feedback. The person(s) providing the barbs will come to serve as discriminative stimuli for anger control and can take the opportunity to prompt and reinforce the adolescent for self-controlled behavior in the natural environment (Peterson, 1983).

Nontransfer of Training: How to Detect and Remediate It

Setbacks (such as losing one's temper) are inevitable, especially when the adolescent continues to live in the environment where the anger control problems developed or were exacerbated. Dysfunctional family systems or residential settings abound with provoking stimuli that will continue to test the adolescent's anger control abilities. The adolescent should be taught to expect these challenges. But if those completing the program return immediately to their previous ways of responding to conflicts, something else may be operating. Feedback from others in the environment as well as from the adolescent should alert the therapist to the reasons for nontransfer. If the adolescent reports not wanting to try self-control or not remembering what is supposed to be done, perhaps the skills have not been adequately learned, or the reinforcers for performing the skills are nonexistent. We recommend analyzing this on an individual basis to determine the need for special generalization strategies.

If booster sessions or establishing cues for anger control in the environment are ineffective, external reinforcements may be required. This would include the provision of reinforcers contingent upon the adolescent's display of particular anger control skills in a naturally occurring conflict. Although this changes the program from pure self-control training, it may be warranted initially. These reinforcers can then be faded on a systematic schedule once control is transferred to self-reinforcement contingencies.

Termination of Treatment

Setting Behavioral Criteria for Termination

Certainly one of the key ways to ensure a successful outcome for the anger control program is to plan carefully for termination. Adolescents should ideally be required to meet preset criteria for self-controlled behavior during interpersonal conflict before graduating from the program. These criteria may be determined relative to the adolescent's own baseline performance (i.e., the average number of conflicts not handled well prior to treatment) or some normative sample. Normative data may be obtained from successful graduates of the program or from some data collection with adolescents not labeled for their anger control disorder. A criterion of at least a 50% reduction in "not handled" conflicts should be required if you have baseline data available. Although this might be possible when working in individual treatment, most groups are conducted with preset lesson plans and are time limited. We have solved this problem by requiring that students not reaching the stated behavioral criteria by the last formal session complete a set of follow-up sessions. If, however, continuous data are not available, there are other sources of evaluation that will help decide if an adolescent is ready to terminate the anger control training.

Probes. The barb assessment method comes in handy. During the last phase of formal training, the adolescent should receive unplanned barbs in a variety of situations. His/her responses should be noted and compared with data from earlier barbs. If there is a significant change (such as a marked decrease in hostile statements or threatening gestures), this indicates that the adolescent has learned the skills and that they have transferred to nontreatment settings.

Videotaped Role Plays. Data from videotaped role plays of conflict situations may also be used to evaluate termination readiness, but this requires preplanning. Tapes must be made prior to the start of treatment and immediately following. Behavioral criteria for each category of responding may be determined based on the individual adolescent's pretraining performance. An example of how these criteria may be stated is:

Termination Criteria for Gerard
At posttest videotaping of conflict scenes involving authority figures, Gerard will have reduced his frequencies of curses, verbal threats, and aggressive physical

responses by 50% relative to his pretest videotape. Further, the loudness of his voice will be rated two points lower than his pretest rating, on a scale of 1–10.

Other Sources of Evaluative Data. If none of these types of objective data are available, termination readiness may be assessed by asking significant others to evaluate the adolescent's behavior change. A simple form may be developed and administered to parents, teachers, counselors, or others, contingent upon the adolescent's approval. Actually, if the adolescent has learned the anger control skills and is applying them to interpersonal conflicts, you will probably be "allowed" to collect this information. Table 5.4 presents a sample evaluation form.

Clinical Decisions

Ideally, adolescents completing the anger control program will exhibit both transfer and maintenance of the skills learned and will have met the preset behavioral criteria for termination. However, there are cases in which decisions concerning termination or the need for a different treatment approach are indicated.

Contraindications for Anger Control. If all of the usual strategies used to enhance skill acquisition and performance have been tried and the adolescent still does not show any improvement in controlling his/her temper, then anger control training may not be the treatment of choice. There may be critical client characteristics (discussed below) that will preclude the acquisition of anger control. Certain adolescents will require more basic social skills or impulse control training as a prerequisite. Further, there may be very powerful reinforcers available, contingent upon temper release and aggressive behavior. Until these are altered, they will supersede any anger control training.

Table 5.4. Anger Control Evaluation Form

Student's Name: _____
Rater's Name: _____
Date: _____ Group No.: _____

1. Have you seen the above named student involved in an interpersonal conflict during the past two weeks? If so, please describe his/her responses _____

2. Have you noticed changes in his/her methods of temper control? If so, in which ways? _____

3. Rate the level of improvement in anger control over the past month

1	2	3	4	5	6	7	8	9
none			some		a good deal			total

4. Would you say that the above named student still needs help in controlling his/her temper and solving interpersonal problems? If so, please describe why:

_____

_____

Individualized Treatment Approaches. Some adolescents may benefit more from only certain program components and in a different order than contained in the formal program. For some, merely the distraction techniques (stop, deep breath, count to five) or the assertion skills may be all that are needed for more effective conflict resolution. Although a formal component analysis has yet to be conducted to determine the most effective strategies contained in the program, the clinician will certainly have some hunches and may terminate following the most effective sections.

In some cases, the decision will be made to postpone termination, based on the adolescent's inconsistent performance of anger control. In this case, certain skills may need to be reemphasized, or the adolescent may need extended role plays with a variety of antagonists to reinforce the learning that has taken place. It is well-known that each individual learns at a different rate, and the pace of the training must reflect this.

Premature Terminations. Finally, there may be well-justified reasons for halting the adolescent's participation in the program before completing all sessions. Some of these reasons include:

1. Student is expelled, suspended, or transferred from school or residential setting.
2. Student experiences major crisis requiring alternate forms of treatment.
3. Student is so disruptive that group sessions are uncontrollable and unproductive.
4. Student refuses to comply with homework (not due to misunderstanding or noncomprehension).
5. Other program changes prevent the student from participating (e.g., placed in seclusion).

If possible, the anger control training should be continued whenever the adolescent is able to participate again. Certain behavioral standards must be set, however, and these might include appropriate group behavior and completion of homework.

REASONS FOR FAILURE OF ANGER CONTROL TRAINING

Although the program described in this manual has been evaluated with various adolescent populations and found to be effective in decreasing aggressive behavior and promoting problem-solving and self-management behaviors, success is not guaranteed, and there will be some treatment failures. These failures, namely adolescents who have not benefited from the program or entire groups that have shown limited progress, have been analyzed and seem to stem from several sources. These are discussed below, along with remediation strategies where applicable.

Failures Due to Client Characteristics

Depending upon the population of adolescents who will receive training, there are several client variables that should be assessed prior to the start of treatment.

Problem: Inadequate Assessment

There are some clients who have severe social skills deficiencies and respond aggressively for lack of other interpersonal skills. These adolescents may not have the accompanying physiological and cognitive components of the anger-arousal cycle and would therefore not benefit from much of the program. Further, these socially deficient clients would require such extensive coaching during role plays that the group process would be significantly impeded. There are also some adolescents who behave quite aggressively, but with no apparent accompanying emotion. For these clients, the aggressive responses have a functional and intentional component and will not be readily abandoned.

Solution

Conduct a careful pretreatment assessment with an extensive analysis of the adolescent's provocation sequence, using instruments that highlight social competence, assertion, and anxiety. Obtain careful descriptions from others about the client's arousal pattern and subsequent responding. Probe for both cognitive and physiological responses. Adolescents who have a history of criminal/delinquent activities, who have strong peer systems (i.e., gang affiliations), or who are able to fully control themselves whenever they decide to can be screened out early on.

Problem: Developmental and Cognitive Deficits

In an excellent review of subject variables affecting self-instructional programs for children, Copeland (1981) indicates that developmental changes in cognitive level and self-regulation will affect responsiveness to cognitive-behavioral treatments. More specifically, younger children who may not spontaneously produce mediating self-verbalizations, clients with lower IQ's, and more cognitively impulsive children will struggle with some of the self-control techniques germane to the program.

Solution

When working with groups, clients having the above characteristics should be grouped together, and there should be extra structure during sessions. Homework assignments must be quite specific and concrete, and anger control skills will need to be prompted and initially reinforced, both in the group and in the natural environment. Further, since evidence suggests that impulsive children respond well to response-cost contingencies (Copeland, 1981), consequences should be arranged for their group behavior, such as attending and participating in role plays, and their homework compliance.

Problem: Lack of Motivation or Resistance to Change

With adolescents, these issues of motivation and resistance are critical to achieving self-control success. According to Peterson (1983), motivation to change involves the degree to which the client identifies with the target program behaviors, the perceived rewards and punishers for altering the behaviors, and the past history of attempts to change the behaviors. Many aggressive adolescents have built up massive resistances in response to the usual external control systems that have attempted to control their behavior. If court contacts, restrictive environments, and other response-cost contingencies have all failed to produce change in the adolescent, then it is almost certain that the resistance to change will be great and the motivation to change almost nonexistent.

Solution

If an adolescent has only a weak commitment to the treatment program or if he/she actively engages in sabotage efforts during the training, the sources of resistance must be analyzed. Many of the variables influencing compliance to treatment, as outlined by Shelton and Levy (1981), are applicable to this analysis and will briefly be reviewed here. Lack of motivation and resistance may be a result of unnecessary fears or negative expectations of behavior change. The adolescent, not knowing exactly which skills he/she will be taught to use during a provocation, may fear the consequences of behaving passively. Certainly, the adolescent may be fearful of the reactions of peers and significant others. Further, if an adolescent has already been the target of numerous intervention programs, he/she may have internalized the failures and be quite doubtful that anything can work to his/her advantage. These fears and negative expectations can be confronted with the adolescent and cleared up prior to treatment. Each adolescent should receive a careful explanation of the skills to be taught, the methods used to teach the new skills, and the success rate of adolescents who have already been through the program. (This might be best done by a program graduate, who would be a realistic role model.) Further, the adolescent will need much support and encouragement when first beginning and when making mistakes. However, if the program is presented in a positive light, as an "opportunity," the adolescent will feel more positive about participation.

Problem: Interfering Attitudes and Beliefs

Related to some of the other subject variables already described, some particular attitudes and beliefs may interfere with the adolescent's commitment to the anger control program. First, there are some strong cultural beliefs that affect a person's handling of aggressive provocations. In some cultures, it is totally unacceptable to walk away from a provoker; in other cultures, aggressive behavior on the part of males is highly regarded. Secondly, there are some attributional styles that seem antagonistic to the anger control objectives. Some adolescents will attribute all causes of behavior to external sources and will not take responsibility for their own behavior and/or behavior change. This makes it difficult to teach self-control skills. Finally, some adolescents have an all-or-none attitude about their behavior and environment. If they try an anger control technique once and it does not work 100%, they will quickly abandon it.

Solution

Cultural beliefs are best handled by a therapist or role model who belongs to the adolescent's culture and is able to control his/her anger without compromising his/her beliefs. Sometimes it is hard to locate such necessary treatment personnel. For attributional and attitudinal styles, some pretraining may enhance the subsequent cognitive-behavioral training (Copeland, 1981). Using problem-solving materials from other sources (e.g., Shure & Spivack, 1972), adolescents can be taught to attribute causes of behavior to more internal sources (within the protagonist in a particular situation and then within themselves). Further, by using a Likert-type scale or facsimile to rate characteristics of a situation, adolescents can be taught to focus on all possible midpoints between the all-or-none anchors viewed previously. An analogy that we have used is temperature which is described as either hot or cold (some may concede to warm). We then structure the labeling of certain scenes or situations with a temperature reading. This can be used in an analogous manner by having the adolescent use a temperature-type scale to measure the "hotness" of particular conflicts or the temperature of his/her anger during provocation. This type of pretraining or extra step during training will help the adolescent who tends to view the extremes alone.

Problem: Interfering Anxiety or Other Psychopathology

Some adolescents, especially those in residential psychiatric facilities, may not be able to fully benefit from the anger control training program because of severe behavioral disturbances in other areas of functioning. High levels of anxiety, manifested in a host of physiological and behavioral symptoms (e.g., tics, stuttering, hyperventilation, shouting, crying, etc.), will certainly prevent the learning and performance of any new skills. Severe depression and possible suicidal ideation, manifested by withdrawn behavior, psychomotor retardation, excessive crying, negative self-statements, and the like, must be attended to prior to focusing on aggressive responding toward others. And finally, adolescents who suffer from psychotic episodes, characterized by hallucination or delusional thinking, will certainly be disruptive to the group teaching format and be unable to comprehend and apply new skills.

Solution

These adolescents must be screened out of the anger control training program until such time as they are better matched to both the inherent content and structure. Sometimes these behavioral disturbances will respond quickly to other forms of therapy, including medication, thus enabling the adolescent to benefit more from anger control training. Sometimes the more disturbed adolescents will benefit from portions of the training program conducted in an individualized manner.

Failures Due to Therapist Characteristics

In addition to certain client variables that may influence response to treatment, there are characteristics of the therapist or trainer that are just as influential.

Problem: Poor Program Presentation

When obtaining a commitment to the program from target adolescents, some therapists fail to present the program in an enthusiastic manner. The therapist who describes the anger control program as a mandatory experience, rather than an opportunity to learn effective self-management skills, imparts a lack of confidence in the training. Further, a therapist whose orientation is not a cognitive-behavioral one may not present the program's philosophy in a positive light.

Solution

Select trainers who have experience with skills training of adolescents and who know the program thoroughly. We suggest that new therapists run through the entire session, planning and practicing all skills themselves, before attempting to work with clients. Also, the verbal description of the program, usually given to adolescents prior to a commitment to participate, should be rehearsed so that it is as positive and realistic as possible.

Problem: Unrealistic Role Models

During individual sessions as well as some group training sessions, the therapist must participate in role plays of conflict situations and model the appropriate anger control skills. Social learning theory (Bandura, 1973) emphasizes that learning via modeling is greatly enhanced by using models with which the clients can identify. The model characteristics that seem most influential are age and sex of model, a "coping" rather than a "mastery" model, and the status or likability of the model. Therapists who are extremely different from the adolescents or who are not liked and respected in a particular agency will struggle to gain compliance to treatment methods and will not serve as effective modeling agents.

Solution

When designating trainers for groups or assigning individual clients, care should be taken to match therapist and client characteristics. Within residential settings, trainers can spend some pretreatment time with target adolescents to establish initial trust and rapport.

Problem: Mechanistic or Boring Teaching Style

Some trainers, especially those who are unfamiliar with the anger control material or who are anxious about running groups of adolescents, will present the material in a rote, inflexible fashion. Following every word in the manual verbatim and conducting the role plays with little drama or enthusiasm is likely to turn the clients off. Further, the trainer must be able to handle the acting-out behavior that will occur during group meetings and role plays without being too controlling.

Solution

Again, care should be taken when designating trainers for adolescents. Enthusiasm, energy, and playfulness are necessary. Trainers should be able to joke with clients, while at the same time imparting the necessary information about particular control techniques. It is our experience that most therapists already know if they feel comfortable and enjoy working with adolescents, and these are the therapists that do the best job.

Failures Due to Inadequacies of Treatment

There are several aspects of the anger control methodology that will influence treatment outcome. These technique variables can be controlled prior to the beginning of the program and need not be a problem.

Problem: Canned Procedures

Clearly, not all adolescents have the same readiness to learn or learn best in the same modality (Peterson, 1983). Further, the group pace may be boring to some and move much too quickly for others. Adhering rigidly to the session-by-session guide may pose problems relative to these individual differences. Also, even though each session contains examples of effective self-statements, they should be used only as examples. Adolescents should be encouraged to generate their own coping and self-evaluative statements.

Solution

These problems are easily solved by providing individualized treatment according to each adolescent's needs and anger control problems. When this is not possible, however, groups should be homogeneously selected according to cognitive functioning and provocation patterns, and the entire group process can be slowed or quickened as necessary. Finally, all therapists should be cautioned *not* to teach the sessions verbatim from the manual. Avoid the use of canned coping statements and the mechanized fashion in which role plays can be conducted. Encourage adolescents to be extremely creative in both the generation of their own self-statements and in acting out interpersonal conflicts.

Problem: Faculty Discrimination

Although most clients will acquire the various anger control skills taught in the group, whether or not they are performed adequately, or in the appropriate situation cannot be guaranteed. Issues of stimulus control are related to the adolescent's ability to discriminate among the stimulus variables and to match his/her responses to the demands of the individual situation. Deciding which anger control skill to use in which situation, when to implement the technique or to use alternate skills, and how to evaluate the impact on the situation require fine-tuned scanning and discrimination skills that are not specifically targeted in the program.

Solution

Initially, discussion of this decision process can be structured along with the evaluation of weekly hassle logs. In determining how well an adolescent handles him/herself during a conflict and what he/she might try next time, these discrimination skills can be prompted. Toward the later phases of the program, we suggest letting the adolescent choose the anger control skill to implement in a particular situation, verbalizing the rationale, and then evaluating the decision following both unsuccessful and successful role plays. Finally, both the spontaneous cuing and barb procedures described in the manual provide opportunities to teach these discrimination and evaluation skills.

Problem: Specific Technique Failures

Although the anger control program presents a specific combination of cognitive-behavioral techniques, it is still an empirical question as to which of the techniques are the most beneficial. Indeed, Bornstein et al. (1981) suggest future research to determine the most effective combination according to specific aggression types and levels of client functioning. For example, some adolescents appear to have a clear anxiety response that often precedes a defensive anger reaction (Novaco, 1975) or that accompanies the inhibitions surrounding the appropriate expression of anger. These clients will benefit from relaxation training and perhaps systematic desensitization prior to the learning of new skills (Elitzur, 1976; Warren & Mchellan, 1982). Other evidence from a component analysis done with impulsive children indicates that the cognitive component of self-instructional training may be most beneficial (Kendall & Braswell, 1982).

Additionally, there may be difficulties in the adolescent's use of specific anger control skills that may contribute to program failure. For example, the self-monitoring of conflict experiences via the hassle log is crucial to the remainder of the program. Unless accurate and complete reporting is done concerning anger provocation events in the adolescent's life, there will be no way to continuously evaluate the adolescent's ability to apply anger control skills. Peterson (1983) and Lipinski and Nelson (1974) have enumerated the following difficulties in the use of self-monitoring methodology:

1. Difficulties in recording the occurrence of problem behaviors or antecedent events due to poor definitions.
2. Deliberate falsification of events.
3. Careless monitoring because it is too time consuming.
4. Competition from other responses, leading to decreased accuracy.
5. Lack of understanding of the rationale and the process of self-monitoring, leading to decreased accuracy and thoroughness.

Solution

These potential problems are best solved by carefully defining each category of the behavior/situational event to be recorded, practicing the process of self-observation and self-recording, simplifying the data sheets, and providing social reinforcement contingent upon complete and accurate recording. Further, it is helpful to role play the self-monitoring process and the potential competing responses or punishers that sometimes surface. For example, the adolescent should role play trying to record in his hassle log while others are still being antagonistic to him/her. Actually, in this situation, the adolescent should be encouraged to store the information necessary in memory until he/she is able to record it on the data sheet.

Failures in the implementation of the self-instructional methodology may also occur. Table 5.5 presents some of the difficulties that may arise with these cognitive techniques.

Table 5.5. Self-Instruction Problems

1. Forgetting the content of reminders.
2. Inability to generate new reminders for new situations.
3. Being too anxious to remember or use the reminders effectively.
4. Poor timing; using reminders too early or too late in terms of the conflict situation and the level of anger.
5. Verbalizing the reminders aloud so that they serve as a provoking stimulus to others involved in the hassle.
6. Using the reminders in a rote or mechanized fashion so that they do not serve as effective control statements.
7. Inability to persist with calming reminders after initial attempts have failed.
8. Failing to implement self-reinforcement reminders following the hassle, regardless of the outcome.
9. Using only pause or calming reminders and failing to self-prompt what action to take in the situation.

Many failures in the use of self-instructions can be prevented through repeated role plays and direct feedback about each of the potential difficulties. Rehearsals of new situations in which there is inappropriate timing, an escalation of conflicts despite the use of self-statements, and unresolved conflicts requiring some kind of positive reinforcement will provide opportunities for the adolescent to expand and strengthen his/her repertoire of coping statements. Role plays should be preceded by the therapist's modeling of the errors, and adolescents should provide feedback and suggestions for improvement. Adolescents usually respond well to this teaching process, whereby they can point out the therapist's mistakes.

Finally, failure in attempts to use some of the other anger control skills (self-reinforcement, self-contracting, assertion, relaxation) may be due to: difficulty in the execution of the response, low payoff for the desired response, history of unsuccessful attempts at anger control, or strong punishment attached to the failure to execute self-control (Peterson, 1983). Each of these failures must be analyzed on an individual basis and remediation efforts planned. In general, it is helpful to remove the threat of past failures by outlining the differences in skills to be learned and by acknowledging the difficulties inherent in any self-change attempt. Further, the actual rather than the anticipated consequences of increased anger control should be emphasized. Remember that adolescents by nature are suspicious of any attempts to change their behavior, and a clear understanding of the rationale and process of the anger control training program is needed. Finally, certain individuals will have problems implementing techniques and may require extra help. For example, group relaxation training may be difficult for some clients, who may require individualized instructions and practice. But not all adolescents will benefit from all techniques anyway, and it is not necessary to "force" the skills.

Problem: Insufficient Treatment

It is certainly possible that adolescents who are participating in the anger control training program will require additional therapeutic services. If you are working in an inpatient setting, there are adjunct therapies already in place and other treatment personnel involved in each adolescent's case. However, on an outpatient basis, these services may not be readily accessible.

Solution

A comprehensive initial assessment must be conducted in order to prioritize the adolescent's treatment needs. Presenting emotional and behavioral problems should be aligned in a hierarchical fashion, so that the most salient difficulties receive immediate attention. The anger control program should be used in many cases as an adjunct to a more conventional therapy plan. The program's structure and its skills-acquisition focus are appropriate for some, but not all adolescents.

Chapter 6
Review and Summary

ANGER CONTROL
PROGRAM SUMMARY

Review of Program Rationale

The anger control training program described in this guidebook has been developed for intervention with adolescents in various settings who display disruptive and aggressive behavior and exhibit poor self-control or impulsive responding. The program is based on the premise that these adolescents have particular behavioral and cognitive skill deficiencies that can be assessed and targeted for remediation. The arousal management and cognitive strategies contained in the program are focused on the control of emotional and impulsive responding and the appropriate expression of anger in an assertive and more rational manner. The training program is appropriate for adolescents in a variety of settings and should be marketed with a focus on skills training and self-control enhancement. Adolescents will actually experience greater satisfaction from effective communication in interpersonal conflicts and from more controlled mood states. Thus the rationale provided to the adolescent is not focused on punishment due to aggressive responding or reducing effective responding to provocation, but rather on increased interpersonal effectiveness.

Review of Anger Control Assessment
and Treatment Methods

Chapter 2 of this book described in detail the numerous assessment devices that are appropriate tools for the evaluation of the anger control intervention. Depending upon the setting for the intervention, certain assessment methods are more practical than others. At the very least, however, we suggest conducting some sort of pre- and postevaluation of the adolescent's self-reported anger and assertion and the behavior changes noted by significant others. An adolescent assertion scale and a teacher/parent behavior checklist would meet these objectives. Further, we suggest continuous data collection by the adolescent via the hassle log format. This not only provides the clinician with ongoing reports of provocation incidents and outcomes, but also allows for continuous feedback to the adolescent and serves as a therapeutic intervention in the development of self-control. Finally, if at all possible, we suggest continuous data collection of actual aggressive behavior in classroom and living environments. Many times this can be done inferentially from already existing sources of data or can be gleaned from persons in the environment who are willing to conduct time sample observations.

Table 6.1 provides a brief overview of each of the anger control techniques presented in this manual and the suggested sequence for intervention. As discussed later in this chapter, however, particular components of the package may be more beneficial than others, and the sequence of components can certainly be altered to fit the needs of the specific adolescent population.

Review of Generalization and Maintenance Strategies

It has been clearly demonstrated that adolescents who receive the anger control training program described in this book exhibit better methods of cognitive problem solving, more assertiveness, and less disruptive classroom and residential behaviors. However, there has currently been insufficient data collection on the generalization and maintenance of learned anger control skills. We strongly urge consideration of these issues prior to treatment initiation. Table 6.2 presents some generalization enhancement strategies.

Finally, in order to promote the long-term maintenance of anger control, booster sessions and follow-up meetings are suggested. These should be preplanned so that the adolescent completing the training program knows when to expect a check on his/her behavior.

Review of Factors Influencing Successful Outcome

In chapter 5, the numerous factors that seem to influence the successful outcome of anger control skills training were reviewed. Clearly, not all of these factors can be attended to, but we suggest at a minimum that the following be done:

1. Conduct a careful client screening and form the treatment groups with a focus on homogeneity and group dynamics.
2. Select trainers who work well with adolescents and who are well-practiced in each of the anger control skills.

Table 6.1. Summary of Anger Control Procedures for Use with Aggressive Adolescents

I. Assessment and analysis of provocation cues and anger responses

    A. Self-monitoring techniques:
        1. Identification of aggressive responses to provocation, antecedent-provoking stimuli, and consequent events.
        2. Self-rating of anger components.
        3. Training in self-recording and compilation of own data.
        4. Analysis of provocation sequences and behavioral patterns.

II. Training of alternative responses to external-provoking stimuli

    A. Self-instructions:
        1. Definition and generation of relevant self-instructions (termed *reminders*)
        2. Modeling and role playing of how and when to use self-verbalizations to guide overt and covert behaviors.
        3. Training both generalized and specific self-instructions.

    B. Self-evaluation skills:
        1. Determination of individual self-evaluating statements that currently function as reinforcers or punishers.
        2. Definition of self-evaluations as a form of self-instruction that provides feedback and guides performance in both resolved and unresolved provocation incidents.

    C. Thinking-ahead techniques:
        1. Presentation of problem-solving strategy designed to help client use the estimation of future negative consequences for misbehavior to guide current responses to provocation.
        2. Modeling and role playing of how and when to use self-generated contingency statements concerning negative consequences.

    D. Relaxation techniques:
        1. Presentation of arousal-management techniques to aid in the identification of physiological responses to provocation and to control muscle tension during or in anticipation of conflicts.
        2. Modeling and rehearsal of deep breathing, active and passive relaxation and imagery.

III. Techniques to control own provocation behaviors

    A. Angry behavior cycle:
        1. Discrimination of own behaviors that may act as provocation cues to others and of escalating sequences of aggression.
        2. Contracting for change infrequency and/or intensity of nonverbal (voice volume, tone, threatening gestures) and/or verbal (threats, arguments, teases) aggressive behaviors that may provoke others.

    B. Assertion without aggression:
        1. Examination of peer pressure, conformity, and conflict with authority issues.
        2. Enumeration of personal rights and responsibilities.
        3. Modeling and role playing of assertion techniques including empathic assertion, fogging, broken record confrontation, minimal assertive response.

Table 6.2. Generalization Enhancement Strategies

1. Use of peers as trainers and generalization cues.
2. Use of generalized self-instructions and problem-solving techniques.
3. *In vivo* homework assignments and barbs.
4. Training in environments other than the therapy setting.
5. Group training that provides more realistic role-play material.
6. Instruction of significant others from the adolescent's environment in the anger control methodology.

3. Schedule the anger control training so as to minimize resistance and aversiveness.
4. Consider the impact of increased anger control on others in the adolescent's environment.
5. Remain flexible in the sequence and method of program presentation; individualize wherever necessary.

Planning a Program Evaluation

Regardless of the setting in which you are conducting adolescent anger control training, an evaluation of the outcome of your treatment efforts is necessary. This may be done in a summative fashion following termination of treatment by assessing behavior change in those receiving the intervention and perceived improvements by significant others in the adolescent's environment. Further, depending on the other data available in the setting, you might analyze the extent to which the program impacted the adolescent in other areas. A consumer-satisfaction type evaluation is also in order. It is important for adolescents to be able to provide feedback about what they liked or didn't like about the program or what aspects they found to be the most constructive. This rather important information should be used to developed improved anger control programs in your setting.

If you have the luxury of being able to conduct clinical research on your adolescent sample, you might evaluate the changes from baseline recording or conduct comparisons with other adolescents receiving different types of treatment. This larger scale program evaluation could be of use in program planning and administrative decision making at an agency-wide level. We have collected follow-up data on over 300 adolescents who have received anger control training at Sagamore Children's Center during the past five years. The majority of these adolescents are either living on their own, with their families, or in group homes and reportedly have exhibited good self-control over impulsive responding. A small number of clients continue to live in restricted environments, since they require further psychiatric treatment or have become involved in the correctional system. These kinds of follow-up data, although anecdotal in nature, are easy to collect and provide an estimate of the long-lasting impact of the anger control program.

CONSIDERATIONS FOR
IMPLEMENTATION IN
VARIOUS SETTINGS

Appropriate Settings for Anger Control Training

Clearly, the anger control intervention package described in this guidebook can be adapted and extended to a variety of clinical and educational settings. The following is a partial listing of settings in which anger control programs have been implemented, both on an individual and group level:

1. private therapy practice
2. outpatient clinics associated with hospitals or community mental health agencies
3. residential facilities: psychiatric hospitals, secure facilities, residential schools, camps
4. community placements: group homes, supportive living facilities, sheltered workshops
5. educational settings: public schools, special education classrooms, resource rooms
6. medical settings: rehabilitation centers, pain management and pediatric units
7. substance abuse programs.

Certainly the content and format of the anger control intervention will depend upon the particular setting and population being served. However, the basic skills training and arousal-management strategies remain the same. In the majority of these settings, the adolescents involved are also receiving other forms of therapy. Care should therefore be taken that there are no contraindications for the anger control program. In general, we recommend that in all settings the entire staff should be apprised of the treatment goals and methods for this program. We have found that this is most effectively accomplished via an in-service training with any and all staff who might be involved with the adolescent. This is a necessary therapeutic as well as precautionary measure. It would be most unfortunate if the adolescent's attempts at anger management were not reinforced.

Issues to Consider in Planning and Implementing Anger Control Interventions

Although the anger control program seems easily adaptable to a variety of settings, there are several potential problem areas that require some forethought.

Administration of the Anger Control Program

Although advertising and marketing concepts are not often applied to clinical endeavors, introducing and selling the anger program require careful planning. There are several levels that require individual strategies. The first is the agency administrative level. If the clinician is already involved with administrative treatment planning, the program can easily be incorporated. We have found it helpful when introducing the program to use videotapes of group sessions, examples of treatment manuals, and published research reports documenting the program's effectiveness. It is important to make sure that the program will not interfere or compete with already existing therapies or therapists. If the clinician does not have administrative support for the program, numerous obstacles will arise along the way. Clear support is needed in order to conduct training, obtain supplies, and involve other relevant people so as to ensure generalization. Certainly, if the clinician is collecting data that may be used to evaluate the program, the administration must approve this.

The staff level is the next to consider when implementing the program. All treatment personnel as well as direct-care staff should be involved in the marketing of the training. This requires a full understanding of program rationale, treatment procedures (especially homework assignments), treatment goals, and the format of program sessions. If staff members are invited to give their feedback on the program and the adolescent participants, and are allowed to participate in some group sessions, this will greatly enhance cooperation and promote generalization of newly acquired skills to extratherapeutic environments.

Finally, the marketing of the program to the adolescents themselves needs careful consideration. Our most successful strategy in both residential and classroom settings has been to give a brief program presentation on the wards or in the classrooms. We show videotapes of group sessions and discuss what the program is designed to teach. The increased personal power rationale is presented, and then we describe successful and unsuccessful graduates of the program. The adolescents then begin to offer their own perceptions of why the program may or may not succeed, and we ask for their voluntary participation. At times, bringing along an actual graduate will be beneficial. Remember to stress the voluntary aspect.

Client Recruitment

If the clinician is working in a residential setting, a captive live-in population with similar behavioral difficulties is available. This greatly facilitates the construction of homogeneous therapy groups. Furthermore, living together usually creates significant anger control problems that can directly benefit from training. In most residential facilities, there are no financial considerations, and adolescents may in fact be motivated to join, since their participation may speed up their release from the residential facility.

Client recruitment is more difficult when working in an outpatient setting or where there are few appropriate adolescents. In these cases, although it may be desirable to conduct group training, it may not be feasible. Clients may be obtained from existing caseloads in the clinic, from outside advertising, or from referrals. This will most probably lead to a heterogeneous group in terms of age, sex, severity of behavior problems, and situations requiring amelioration. Further, on an outpatient basis, there may be scheduling difficulties and increased costs for advertising and client recruitment. Finally, the group approach is not always accepted on the outpatient level, since most clients expect individualized attention. To circumvent this resistance, as well as the usual adolescent resistance to therapy, an individualized anger control treatment program in conjunction with additional therapeutic interventions may be helpful.

We have suggested (Feindler et al., 1984a) that the best advertisement for anger control training comes from conducting inservice sessions for potential referral sources. Anger control presentations are most welcomed by teachers, social workers, psychologists, and the like. Further, a free orientation session for professionals as well as for parents and their adolescent children might also help to recruit participants.

Competing Contingencies

An analysis of any and all environmental contingencies that might influence the adolescent's treatment program or administrative support must be undertaken prior to program implementation. Although this takes time and thought, it is necessary to ensure program success. For the adolescent, competing contingencies might include:

1. parental involvement or support
2. residential release requirements
3. peer norms and culture
4. severe behavior problems in other areas
5. involvement in outside activities
6. other therapeutic goals and strategies
7. potential punishments/response cost for noncontrolled anger

All of these factors may influence attainment of the anger control program's therapeutic goals. Most of them can be incorporated into the training program and used to reinforce the adolescent's progress (e.g., parent and peer involvement and institutional rewards contingent upon behavioral improvement). However, some factors (e.g., other behavioral disturbances, substance abuse, gang membership) may operate to undermine benefits accruing from the training. At the very least, these factors must be investigated and attempts made to control those that will block optimum treatment gain.

Generalization Planning

Included in this guidebook are numerous suggestions for transfer and maintenance strategies. We have stressed the importance of planning so that gains made in anger management generalize across time and to other environments. However, these suggestions are more easily implemented in some settings than others. Clearly, in residential settings, the trainers have unlimited access to adolescents for follow-up and booster sessions. Staff training and parent sessions can be easily arranged at no extra cost. These persons can then serve as discriminative stimuli for appropriate anger control in the natural setting and can prompt and reinforce necessary strategies. Further, the adolescent's resumption of earlier explosive response styles can be identified and dealt with promptly. Finally, an obstacle to generalization for training in residential settings is the limited access adolescents have to real-world problems and free choice situations. This is the most stringent generalization test.

In outpatient settings and/or settings in which the anger program has not received unanimous support, the scheduling of follow-up or booster sessions is difficult. Further, parent and staff involvement with the actual training program is minimal and, if required, is an additional expense. Also, although the adolescents in outpatient facilities are coping with real-world hassles and have significantly more options in terms of their behavioral responses, the trainers and those in the group sessions will have limited access to *in vivo* occurrences of the provocation events. They must rely solely on the adolescent's self-report of improved anger control. This can be approximated with the barb procedure suggested earlier. Finally, we suggest (Feindler et al., 1984a) that program manuals be developed for parents and teachers and anger control training be conducted in the naturalistic environment (classroom, park, etc.).

FUTURE APPLICATIONS OF ANGER
CONTROL INTERVENTIONS

Extensions to Other Populations

The anger control training program described in this manual has been implemented and evaluated in a variety of settings for adolescents. Successful outcomes have been reported in an inpatient psychiatric setting (Feindler et al., 1986), a residential classroom setting (Feindler et al., 1984b), and outpatient adolescent groups (Feindler et al., 1984a). Certainly there are numerous other settings and populations that would benefit from an extension and perhaps a modification of the cognitive-behavioral anger control techniques.

Substance Abusers

Adolescents who have drug and/or alcohol dependencies are often engaged in delinquent activities in the buying, selling, or using of the substance and are faced with conflict situations surrounding drug usage. Further, it may be that adolescents use these substances to help them cope with difficult situational demands. Unfortunately, this type of coping is rarely considered adaptive or effective, and in actuality, the use of such substances may disinhibit patterns of aggression. These adolescents exhibit marked skill deficiencies in self-control, problem solving, and conflict negotiation and would certainly benefit from the anger management skills of relaxation, assertion, self-instruction, and the like.

There is only one reported investigation of anger control training for a substance abuse population. Schrader et al. (1977) presented Novaco's (1975) stress inoculation package to six adolescents with histories of soft drug usage. Following the five-session treatment, those adolescents had reduced frequencies of verbal aggression and disruptive classroom behavior. Certainly, the implementation of training with this population would require some modifications of the techniques and training format. The content of role plays would need to emphasize the conflicts surrounding drug usage, peer pressure to conform, or the inability to refuse drug offers. This would also help these adolescents to cope with stressful interpersonal conflicts. Moreover, the role of the drug in the provocation cycle would require detailed analysis, and the adolescent would need practice in implementing more adaptive coping skills. Self-monitoring procedures would also have to include an assessment of the urge to use substances and the actual use of substances. It is strongly recommended that adolescents be drug-free when receiving anger control training. Adolescents under the influence of drugs will not only be unable to retain information, but they will be highly disruptive to the group process as well.

Correctional Facilities

Since the primary rehabilitation modality used for delinquent adolescents has been incarceration in a closed facility, it seems most appropriate to extend anger control training to this setting. Conflict situations abound in a setting with strong punishment contingencies and many behavior rules. In addition, when delinquents are contained in a small environment together, there is frequent interpersonal conflict. Schlichter and Horan (1981) conducted stress inoculation training with 38 adjudicated male delinquencies in a correctional facility. Compared to a control condition, those adolescents receiving therapy evidenced lower rates of verbal aggression in role-play provocations and on self-report inventories. Table 6.3 presents their streamlined adaptation of anger control training.

In a forensic setting, Stermac (1984) presented Novaco's stress inoculation approach to 30 male adult offenders with lengthy criminal and psychiatric histories. Preliminary results indicated reductions in aggressive responding on self-report measures and on impulsivity during a cognitive task. Unfortunately, no direct behavioral observations or follow-up data were reported.

In extending the anger control methodology to a population of adolescent offenders, certain changes in the program structure and format may be required. First, a decision should be carefully made as to whether a group format is manageable. Certainly role plays would more closely approximate conflicts occurring in the correctional facility, but an individualized approach that is relevant to the particular offender's history, terms of sentence, and future plans may be more effective. Completion of homework assignments may be limited, since the facilities'

Table 6.3. A Six-Step Anger Control Coping Strategy

1. Recognition of aggression-eliciting situations in one's history.
2. Preparation for such events via self-instruction to remain calm.
3. Continuation of self-instruction to remain calm when actually confronting the provocation.
4. Utilization of autonomic responses as cues to employ one or more coping skills to reduce the intensity of angry feelings (e.g., relaxation, backward counting, pleasant imagery).
5. Exhibition of an assertive (not aggressive) response.
6. Self-reinforcement for effectively handling the situation.

rules of conduct and punishment are primary. Furthermore, the inmates' motivation to participate in the training may be based on avoidance of work and/or relief from boredom and not on willingness to make changes. Since the inmates' motivation and ability to make desired behavioral changes will have little influence on their current internment, future consequences of more controlled responding must be highlighted. Finally, given the severity of aggressive behavior and other antisocial behavior patterns, the impact of anger and self-control may be minimal.

Family Anger Control Training

The behavioral literature abounds with examples of successful parent training programs for various populations of children with behavior disorders. However, there are few investigations targeted at parents of adolescents and at cognitive-behavioral self-control strategies. The family problem-solving techniques developed by Blechman and colleagues (Blechman, Taylor, & Schrader, 1981) seem well suited to teaching parents and adolescents together the skills required for successful conflict negotiation. Additionally, use of the communication skills training approach developed by Robin and colleagues (Robin, 1981; Robin & Foster, 1984; Robin, Kent, O'Leary, Foster, & Prinz, 1977) can result in fewer parent-adolescent clashes and improved problem solving in regard to typical conflict situations. Whether these problems would be easily adaptable to adolescents with delinquent or aggressive behavioral histories or to families with adolescents who are incarcerated or hospitalized remains to be seen. But clearly, the families of these adolescents are an underserved population who most probably exhibit poor anger control themselves.

There have been recent investigations of extensions of behavioral parent training to child abusing parents who are usually characterized as having poor impulse and anger control. Parents receiving training in human development, child management, problem solving, and self-control showed improved child management skills as measured in home observations and on self-report inventories (Wolfe, Kaufman, Aragona, & Sandler, 1981; Wolfe, Sandler, & Kaufman, 1981). Denicola and Sandler (1980) also reported similar improvements with abusive parents who were exposed to a more cognitive-behavioral training program. More recently there has been a report on the positive effects of Novaco's anger control methodology with abusive parents (Nomellini & Katz, 1983).

A family anger control training program, designed for use with a variety of adolescent populations and their parents, appears to be an appropriate extension of the methodology. A combination of the content and formats of the above-described family interventions and of the anger management techniques known to be effective with adults and adolescents might reduce the incidence of family conflict and of individual patterns of aggressive behavior.

Similar to the negotiation training reported by Kifer et al. (1974), parents and adolescents would receive instructions, practice, and feedback about both hypothetical and actual conflict situations. Coaching of the implementation of all of the cognitive-behavioral anger control skills should be done in the treatment environment; then skills should be coached both in the treatment environment and *in vivo* in the home. All family members should be required to self-monitor relevant data across time (i.e., number of conflicts, antecedent and consequent events, urges to be aggressive, angry feelings, etc.). If an adolescent is in an inpatient setting, this type of program should be started well in advance of his/her release. Family groups or individual treatment may both be beneficial; however, the individualized approach seems the best.

Anger Control Training for Professionals and Paraprofessionals

Aggressive adolescents often come into contact with school and mental health professionals, community professionals, and paraprofessionals. The behavior patterns of these adolescents may elicit angry and/or aggressive reactions on the part of these people and may create a conflict interaction. This not only reinforces the adolescent's initial explosive behavior, but provides adult models of aggression and condones aggressive responses to these stressful interpersonal interactions. It is also the case that mental health personnel as well as law enforcement officials have high levels of job stress and burnout and may be more likely to respond angrily to provocation. In order to help the adolescent achieve self-control competence, these adults may benefit from anger management training.

There have been several reports of this type of intervention with law enforcement officers (Novaco, 1977b; Rahaim et al., 1980), probation counselors (Novaco, 1980), and childcare workers (Feindler et al., 1980). Novaco (1977b) presented a comprehensive stress-inoculation program that emphasized cognitive determinants of anger arousal and methods for coping with provocation. This program was geared toward the police officers' self-control, while training of probation counselors (Novaco, 1980) emphasized dealing with clients having problems with anger and aggression. Counselors received training in preventive, regulatory, and executional anger control skills. They then could instruct their own clients in anger management and in the development of behavioral skills needed to manage provocation experiences. Data from self-report measures and an unannounced role play indicated improved skills and more extensive knowledge of anger-arousal concepts in the training group as compared to a control group.

Related more to personnel having direct involvement with delinquent and explosive adolescents, Feindler et al. (1980) developed a training program for childcare staff. In residential settings, it is well-known that the childcare staff spends the most time with adolescents and has on-line responsibility for management of explosive behavior. It seems that the most effective trainers of anger reduc-

tion methods would be the childcare workers when one considers the following:
- their proximity to occurrences of aggressive behavior on a continual basis
- their role in managing the provocation incident and in administering behavioral consequences
- the possibilities to model and coach appropriate self-control behaviors *in vivo*

Three 1-hour training workshops were conducted with childcare workers in a residential psychiatric center for children and adolescents. Following these didactic presentations on anger management, trainers were available on the wards for certain hours during a 4-week period. They modeled and coached appropriate interventions with angry/aggressive adolescents. Data were obtained on 20 adolescents during a 9-week baseline and an 8-week treatment phase. Figure 6.1 indicates decreases in the frequencies of unit restrictions for physical aggression for the ward in which childcare staff received training. Additionally, self-report data from childcare workers indicated a 20% decrease in stress related to daily job tasks and an increase in the scope and number of written solutions offered to hypothetical on-ward incidents. Certainly this type of intervention (didactic and *in vivo* coaching) is cost-efficient and effective in producing on-ward changes. Unfortunately, it was not possible to collect direct observation data on the childcare workers themselves, so we could not evaluate exactly what they were doing differently. This line of research merits further investigation.

Finally, the focus of the training itself seemed to take two directions: self-management of the childcare worker's anger and teaching the adolescent how to control his/her anger. Although the concepts and strategies are the same, content and teaching methods will differ. It is important to distinguish between these two directions and also to intervene at both levels.

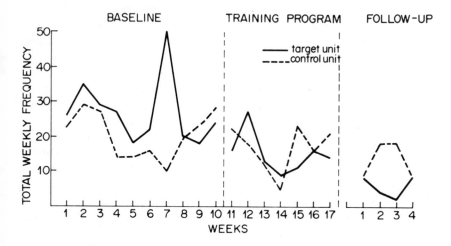

FIGURE 6.1. Frequency of unit restrictions for hitting following staff anger control training

In summary, there is room for significant program development and evaluation in the area of anger control strategies for those mental health, educational, and community personnel who work with aggressive adolescents. It may be quite cost efficient to train them in effective anger management, thus modeling the skills to the adolescent and preventing an escalation of interpersonal conflicts. Anger control training for teachers, psychologists, counselors, and correctional staff seems an appropriate extension of the technology.

Alternative Teaching Formats

It is a known fact that not all of us learn new concepts and skills in the same fashion. Unfortunately, it has been primarily the educators of adolescents who have taken this into account, rather than those involved in therapeutic interventions. Although the anger control program described in this book includes a suggested teaching format, alternative formats should be considered, depending upon the population of adolescents, the setting in which the training will be conducted, and the availability of materials.

Media Techniques

Most therapy interventions are presented to the target clients in the auditory mode; things are explained, and instructions for behavior change are given verbally. Behavioral interventions often include practice components, since skills acquisition most readily occurs with *in vivo* shaping and practice of the target skills. However, there may be certain adolescents who require more of a visual presentation of conceptual information and skills to be modeled. We have found this to be true with adolescents who have certain cognitive deficiencies (such as poor auditory memory and sequencing skills). For these populations, we have incorporated the extensive use of video media and visual prompts into the training program. Initially, the video equipment was used to film role-played provocation incidents in order to analyze the components of the interaction and their sequence. The visual display also provided an opportunity to structure and coach descriptive feedback. These media techniques were supplemented with visual reminders, which served to prompt the appropriate use of anger control strategies in the natural environment. These included stickers showing refrigerators or polar bears (to indicate "chill-out"), index cards with a short list of self-reminders, hand signals from others who had already completed the training program, and finally the "Chill-Out" t-shirts.

In order to further reinforce learning in this modality, we then developed a series of structured videotapes to accompany the usual training format. The tapes, enacted by actual childcare staff, depicted usual ward conflicts and highlighted both the "wrong" and "right" way of handling the conflict. Specific techniques were modeled, and an audiodub indicated to the viewer the technique that was being used. Of course, the outcome of the situation was much more positive for the protagonist, who displayed appropriate anger control strategies. In general, however, the videotapes presented coping models rather than mastery models (Bandura, 1973). Although there has been no empirical evaluation as of yet on this teaching strategy for anger control, anecdotal data indicate that there was better retention of anger control information and increased probability of skill acquisition. In fact, we seem to have capitalized on a preferred activity of adolescents, namely, television viewing, and have turned it into an effective therapeutic adjunct.

Integration Into Classroom Curricula

Since the majority of adolescents who would benefit from this anger control training are under the age of 18, they must also be involved with an educational program. Given the structure and content of the program, it is easily suited to classroom adaptation. This form of intervention may hold promise because adolescents exhibit somewhat less resistance to teaching formats than to therapy formats. Moreover, if an entire class is exposed to the program as part of their affective education, there will be less stigmatization regarding the "need" for such an intervention. And finally, teachers, whether they are "subject" teachers or special educators, are certainly equipped with the skills necessary for teaching effective anger control intervention.

Indeed, there have been several investigations of the integration of behavioral strategies for self-control and problem solving with the educational curriculum objectives. Sanchez-Craig (1976) provided training to seventh and eighth graders who desired an improvement in relationships. During weekly group sessions, students were taught cognitive and behavioral strategies for reappraising stressful social situations. Results indicated a decrease in reported aversiveness of social cues and an increase in alternative responses generated to problem situations. In a large-scale investigation, Sarason and Sarason (1981) used modeling and role-play techniques to teach cognitive and social skills to 127 ninth-grade students as part of their health class curriculum. Students were taught how to approach problem situations, deal with peer pressure, ask for help, and present themselves appropriately in work and school situations. Subjects showed improvement on these target behaviors and evidenced lower rates of tardiness, school absences, and behavior referrals. The authors indicate that the presentation of behavioral skills training in this format was a cost-effective way to approach the prevention of socialization problems. This conclusion is also offered by Filipczak et al. (1980), who presented a group-oriented social skills training program to over 500 junior high school students. The program was presented as a regularly scheduled class in the junior high curriculum and emphasized problem-solving skills, behavior management strategies, social skills, and study skills. Volunteer counselors and teachers received training in the program curriculum and behavioral teaching strategies. Course materials in both printed and audiotaped versions were prepared. Program evaluation results indicated improvements in school attendance, classroom performance, teacher ratings of social skills, and self-control, as compared to control groups.

Finally, a recent investigation revealed another interesting integration of educational and therapeutic objectives with disruptive junior high school students. Brigham et al. (1985) developed a self-management class that ran for six weeks. Using the educational format, students received instruction in the concepts and principles of applied behavior analysis and were required to complete a self-management project. Results indicated that following the training, 103 treatment subjects evidenced lower rates of detentions given for in-school disruptive behavior, improved teacher ratings of school behavior, and increases in knowledge of behavioral principles. Clearly, these large-scale programs, integrated into the traditional educational structure and curricula and easily evaluated via school measures, are cost effective in the remediation of school behavior problems and in the prevention of more severe behavioral difficulties. Unfortunately, there was no attempt made to assess the generalization of these skills training programs to other environments or to other response classes. But we can assume that general cognitive problem-solving strategies and self-management skills are easily transferred to other problem situations.

The anger control training program described in this book could be adapted for use as an educational program and incorporated into the health or human development classes offered in most high schools. The arousal-management strategies (relaxation, deep breathing, imagery, etc.), cognitive-reappraisal strategies, and problem-solving, self-control, and assertive skills could be presented via role plays and modeling (live or video) in classroom settings. Homework assignments and self-monitoring requirements could also be adapted to this setting. Providing anger control training as part of the standard affective curricula will circumvent much of the adolescent's resistance to therapy and will reduce the social stigma of being in therapy. In addition, since most of the provocation incidents involve several youngsters, teaching a whole class to manage their anger effectively seems much more cost efficient. However, since there is a loss of the individualized nature of training, this type of format is not suggested for adolescents with severe behavioral disturbances, those with interfering pathologies, or those who are highly distractible. Finally, in a classroom setting, there will be a loss of the small group interaction so beneficial and necessary to some adolescents. Those with social anxiety may participate and learn more in a smaller group.

Peer Tutoring

Another promising and cost-effective approach to behavioral clinical interventions is peer-mediated intervention. In a review of the recent literature, Kalfus (1984) indicates that peers function well as tutors, reinforcing agents, and facilitators of generalization. Peers who are involved in direct forms of mediation evidence significant behavioral improvements themselves (learning by teaching). Because of this, it would seem that the anger control program could benefit in several ways by incorporating peer trainers.

First, those peers selected as intervention agents would be required to learn and model appropriate anger control skills, both in the therapy session and in other environments. This would certainly enhance the peer trainers' skills and provide additional cues for appropriate anger control. Also, it is well-known that modeling techniques are enhanced when the model and the observer are similar, not only in observable attributes but in behavioral history. An angry adolescent who has learned to control his/her anger and thus cope more effectively with provocation is a more appropriate model than a clinician who has learned how to teach the technology.

Further, the use of peer trainers would facilitate generalization in extratherapeutic environments, since peers would serve both as cues and as reinforcing agents for appropriate anger control. This seems critical. The therapist is usually not available on the basketball court or in the showers where the peer tutors might be! Peers are certainly closer to the actual provocation incidents and thus can provide information concerning the nature of adolescent conflict as well as feedback on the effectiveness of various suggested techniques. These peer trainers can be quite helpful in informal program evaluation.

Finally, since we know that peer contingencies as well as group norms are quite influential in adolescent groups, it behooves the clinician to accept this fact and to incorporate it into the treatment programs. We have found that graduates of the anger control program are the best promoters of the program. By incorporating peer trainers into the methodology, the validity of the training is emphasized in the eyes of the adolescent.

Optimizing the Client to Treatment Match

This book has included many different anger control skills that will help the adolescent to manage his/her anger and achieve better self-control during problematic or stressful interactions. Clearly, each adolescent has a particular repertoire of responses that, when analyzed, will reveal specific skill deficits and assets. Not all adolescents need training in all anger control skills. In the hopes of streamlining the treatment package and providing more efficient treatment, component analysis research is needed. Each component of the treatment package (e.g., relaxation training, self-instructions, assertion) needs to be administered and evaluated separately. In this manner, it could be determined which techniques or skills are most effective in discrete behavior change and in which sequence. Certainly, these component analyses would require replication in different settings and with different populations of adolescents, but the outcome would direct future anger control training efforts. It may be that certain aspects of the skills training are redundant or not necessary or that a particular sequence of training enhances skill development.

Further, research regarding the effectiveness of different techniques with various clinical subtypes of adolescents must be conducted. Although the majority of our anger control training has been directed at adolescents with diagnoses of conduct disorder or oppositional disorder, we do not know enough about particular sets of behavioral disturbances or the histories of adolescents who respond to the training. It may be that there are clear indications and contraindications for anger control training in the adolescent's psychiatric profile or behavioral history. Adolescents who exhibit hyperactive behaviors or attention-deficit disorders may require relaxation training early in the program, whereas another adolescent might require assertion training as the first component. All of these are issues that require future research.

In addition to the need for analyses on the content level, analyses of the effectiveness of different training methods are required. We have included much in our discussion about alternate forms of information presentation, alternate anger control teachers and models, and alternate structures (group versus individual; classroom versus therapy). Much comparative research is required to determine which adolescents in which settings benefit from each of these different methods of anger control training. In this way, we can further optimize treatment gains for the adolescents we are serving.

Finally, we have yet to evaluate the effectiveness of anger control training when combined with other therapeutic interventions. In much of the research to date (Feindler et al., 1983, 1986), anger control training has been provided along with already existing contingency management programs. These different interventions require comparison. In addition, most of the adolescents who have received anger control training are also receiving alternate forms of therapy, such as psychodynamic, family, and medication therapy, as well. Much like the research described by Henshaw, Henker, and Whalen (1984), in which anger control and medication were evaluated separately in hyperactive and aggressive boys, large-scale comparisons as well as individual subject investigations are greatly needed.

References

Achenbach, T. M., & Edelbrock, C. S. (1979). The child behavior profile: II. Boys aged 12-16 and girls aged 6-11 and 12-16. *Journal of Consulting and Clinical Psychology, 47*, 223-233.

Adelson, J. (1980). *Handbook of adolescent psychology*. New York: Wiley Interscience.

Akamatsu, T. J., & Farudi, P. A. (1978). Effect of model status and juvenile offender type on the initiation of self-reward criteria. *Journal of Consulting and Clinical Psychology, 46*, 187-188.

Alexander, R., Corbett, T., & Snigel, J. (1976). The effects of individual and group consequences on school attendance and curfew violators with predelinquent adolescents. *Journal of Applied Behavior Analysis, 9*, 221-226.

Anderson, L., Fodor, I., & Alpert, M. (1976). A comparison of methods for training self-control. *Behavior Therapy, 7*, 649-658.

Bandura, A. (1973). *Aggression: A social learning analysis*. Englewood Cliffs, NJ: Prentice-Hall.

Barenborm, C. (1977). Developmental changes in the interpersonal cognitive system from middle childhood to adolescence. *Child Development, 48*, 1467-1474.

Barkley, R. A., Hastings, J. E., Tousel, R. E., & Tousel, S. E. (1976). Evaluation of a token system for juvenile delinquents in a residential setting. *Journal of Behavior Therapy and Experimental Psychiatry, 7*, 227-230.

Beck, S., Forehand, R., Neeper, R., & Baskin, C. (1982). A comparison of two analogue strategies for assessing children's social skills. *Journal of Consulting and Clinical Psychology, 50*(4), 596-597.

Bellack, A. S., & Hersen, M. (1984). *Research methods in clinical psychology*. New York: Pergamon Press.

Bellack, A., Hersen, M., & Lamparski, P. (1979). Roleplay tests for assessing social skills: Are they valid? Are they useful? *Journal of Consulting and Clinical Psychology, 47*, 335-342.

Besalel, V. A., & Azrin, N. H. (1981). The reduction of problems by reciprocity counseling. *Behavior Research and Therapy, 19*(4), 297-301.

Bistline, J. L., & Frieden, F. P. (1984). Anger control: A case study of a stress inoculation treatment for a chronic aggressive patient. *Cognitive Therapy and Research, 8*(5), 551-556.

Blakely, C. H., & Davidson, W. S., III. (1984). Behavioral approaches to delinquency: A review. In P. Karoly & J. J. Steffen (Eds.), *Adolescent behavior disorders: Foundations and contemporary concerns*. Lexington, MA: Lexington Books/D.C. Heath & Co.

Blechman, E. A., Taylor, C. J., & Schrader, S. M. (1981). Family problem solving vs. home notes as early intervention with high risk children. *Journal of Consulting and Clinical Psychology, 49*, 919-926.

Bornstein, M., Bellack, A. S., & Hersen, M. (1980). Social skills training for highly aggressive children. *Behavior Modification, 4*(2), 173-186.

Bornstein, P. H. (1985). Self-instructional training: A commentary and state of the art. *Journal of Applied Behavior Analysis, 18*, 69-72.

Bornstein, P. H., Hamilton, S. B., & McFall, M. E. (1981). Modification of adult aggression: A critical review of theory, research, and practice. In M. Hersen, R. M. Eisler, & P. M. Miller (Eds.), *Progress in behavior modification: Volume 12*. New York: Academic Press.

Bornstein, P. H., Rychtarik, R. G., McFall, M. E., Bridgwater, C. A., Guthuer, L., & Anton, B. (1980). Behaviorally specific report cards and self-determined reinforcements: A multiple baseline analysis of inmate offenses. *Behavior Modification, 4*, 71–81.

Brigham, T. A., Hopper, C., Hill, B., DeArmas, A., & Newsom, P. (1985). A self-management program for disruptive adolescents in the school: A clinical replication analysis. *Behavior Therapy, 16*(1), 99–115.

Burchard, J. D., & Lane, T. W. (1984). Crime and delinquency. In A. Bellack, M. Hersen, & A. Kazdin (Eds.), *International handbook of behavior modification and therapy*. New York: Plenum.

Camp, B. W. (1977). Verbal mediation in young aggressive boys. *Journal of Abnormal Psychology, 86*, 145–153.

Camp, B. W., Blum, G., Hebert, F., van Doornick, W. (1977). "Think-Aloud": A program for developing self-control in young aggressive boys. *Journal of Abnormal Child Psychology, 5*, 152–169.

Camp, B. W., & Ray, R. S. (1984). Aggression. In A. W. Meyers & W. E. Craighead (Eds.), *Cognitive behavior therapy with children*. New York: Plenum.

Collingwood, T. R., & Genter, R. W. (1980). Skills training as treatment for juvenile delinquents. *Professional Psychology, 11*, 591–598.

Connor, J. M., Dann, L. N., & Twentyman, C. T. (1982). A self-report measure of assertiveness in young adolescents. *Journal of Clinical Psychology, 38*(1), 101–106.

Copeland, A. P. (1981). The relevance of subject variables in cognitive self-instructional programs for impulsive children. *Behavior Therapy, 12*, 520–529.

Copeland, A. P. (1982). Individual difference factors in children's self-management: Toward individualized treatments. In P. Karoly & F. H. Kanfer (Eds.), *Self-management and behavior change: From theory to practice* (pp. 207–239). New York: Pergamon Press.

Copeland, A. P., & Hammel, R. (1981). Subject variables in cognitive self-instructional training. *Cognitive Therapy and Research, 5*, 405–420.

Cormier, W. H., & Cormier, L. S. (1979). *Interviewing strategies for helpers: A guide to assessment, treatment, and evaluation*. Monterey, CA: Brooks/Cole Publishing Co.

Deluty, R. H. (1979). Children's action tendency scale: A self-report measure of aggressiveness, assertiveness and submissiveness in children. *Journal of Consulting and Clinical Psychology, 47*, 1061–1071.

Denicola, J., & Sandler, J. (1980). Training abusive parents in cognitive-behavioral techniques. *Behavior Therapy, 11*, 263–270.

Dishion, T. J., Loeber, R., Stouthamer-Loeber, M., & Patterson, G. (1984). Skills deficits and male adolescent delinquency. *Journal of Abnormal Child Psychology, 12*(1), 37–54.

Dodge, K. A., & Frame, C. L. (1982). Social cognitive biases and deficits in aggressive boys. *Child Development, 53*, 620–635.

Dodge, K. A., & Murphy, R. R., (1984). The assessment of social competence in adolescents. In P. Karoly & J. J. Steffen (Eds.), *Adolescent behavior disorders: Foundations and contemporary concerns*. Lexington, MA: Lexington Books/D.C. Heath & Co.

D'Zurilla, T., & Goldfried, M. (1971). Problem solving and behavior modification. *Journal of Abnormal Psychology, 8*, 107–126.

Elder, J. P., Edelstein, B. A., & Narick, M. M. (1979). Adolescent psychiatric patients: Modifying aggressive behavior with social skills training. *Behavior Modification, 3*(2), 161–178.

Elitzur, B. (1976). Self-relaxation program for acting-out adolescents. *Adolescence, 11*, 569–572.

Ellis, A. (1977). Can we change thoughts by reinforcement? A reply to Howard Rachlin. *Behavior Therapy, 8*, 666–672.

Empy, L. T. (1982). *American delinquency: Its meaning and construction.* Homewood, IL: Dorsey Press.

Emshoff, J. G., Redd, W. H., & Davidson, W. S. (1976). Generalization training and the transfer of treatment effects with delinquent adolescents. *Journal of Behavior Therapy and Experimental Psychology, 7,* 141–144.

Fehrenbach, P. A., & Thelen, M. H. (1982). Behavioral approaches to the treatment of aggressive disorders. *Behavior Modification, 6*(4), 465–497.

Feindler, E. L. (1979). *Cognitive and behavioral approaches to anger control training in explosive adolescents.* Unpublished doctoral dissertation, West Virginia University.

Feindler, E. L., Ecton, R. B., & Kaufman, K. (1984a). *Issues in group anger control training.* Paper presented at Association for Advancement of Behavior Therapy, Philadelphia, PA.

Feindler, E. L., Ecton, R. B., Kingsley, D., & Dubey, D. (1986). Group anger control training for institutionalized psychiatric male adolescents. *Behavior Therapy, 17,* 109–123.

Feindler, E. L., & Fremouw, W. J. (1983). Stress inoculation training for adolescent anger problems. In D. Meichenbaum & M. E. Jaremko (Eds.), *Stress reduction and prevention.* New York: Plenum.

Feindler, E. L., Latini, J., Nape, K., Romano, J., & Doyle, J. (1980). *Training child care workers in anger reduction methods to reduce aggressive incidents in delinquents.* Paper presented at the Association for Advancement of Behavior Therapy, New York.

Feindler, E. L., Marriott, S. A., & Iwata, M. (1984b). Group anger control training for junior high school delinquents. *Cognitive Therapy and Research, 8*(3), 299–311.

Fensterheim, H., & Baer, J. (1975). *Don't say yes when you want to say no.* New York: David McKay Co.

Filipczak, J., Archer, M., & Friedman, R. (1980). In-school social skills training: Use with disruptive adolescents. *Behavior Modification, 4*(2), 243–263.

Finch, A. J., & Eastman, E. S. (1983). A multi-method approach to measuring anger in children. *Journal of Psychology, 115,* 55–60.

Finch, A. J., Saylor, C. F., & Nelson, W. M. (1983). *The children's inventory of anger: A self-report inventory.* Paper presented at the American Psychological Association, Anaheim, CA.

Fixsen, D. L., Phillips, E. L., Dowd, T. P., & Palma, L. J. (1981). Preventing violence in residential treatment programs for adolescents. In R. B. Stuart (Ed.), *Violent behavior: Social learning approaches to prediction, management, and treatment.* New York: Brunner/Mazel.

Fixsen, D. L., Phillips, E. L., & Wolf, M. M. (1972). Achievement place: The reliability of self-reporting and peer reporting and their effects on behavior. *Journal of Applied Behavior Analysis, 5,* 19–30.

Forman, S. G. (1980). A comparison of cognitive training and response cost procedure in modifying aggressive behavior of elementary school children. *Behavior Therapy, 11,* 594–600.

Forman, S. G. (1980). Self-statements of aggressive and non-aggressive children. *Child Behavior Therapy, 2,* 49–57.

Foster, S. L., Prinz, R. J., & O'Leary, K. D. (in press). Impact of problem solving communication training and generalization procedures on family conflict. *Child and Family Behavior Therapy.*

Frederiksen, L. W., & Eisler, R. M. (1977). The control of explosive behavior: A skill development approach. In D. Upper (Ed.), *Perspectives in behavior therapy.* Kalamazoo, MI: Behaviordelia.

Frederiksen, L. W., Jenkins, J. D., Foy, D. W., & Eisler, R. M. (1976). Social skills training to modify abusive verbal outbursts in adults. *Journal of Applied Behavior Analysis, 9,* 117–125.

Freedman, B. J., Rosenthal, L., Donahoe, C. P., Schlundt, D. G., & McFall, R. M. (1978). A social-behavioral analysis of skills deficits in delinquent and non-delinquent adolescent boys. *Journal of Consulting and Clinical Psychology, 46*(6), 1448–1462.

Gaffney, L. R., & McFall, R. M. (1981). A comparison of social skills in delinquent and non-delinquent adolescent girls using a behavioral roleplaying inventory. *Journal of Consulting and Clinical Psychology, 49*(6), 959–967.

Garrison, S. R., & Stolberg, A. L. (1983). Modification of anger in children by affective imagery training. *Journal of Abnormal Child Psychology, 11*(1), 115–129.

Geen, R. G., Stonner, D., & Shope, G. L. (1975). The facilitation of aggression by aggression: Evidence against the catharsis hypothesis. *Journal of Personality and Social Psychology, 31*(4), 721–726.

Goldstein, A. P. (1983). Behavior modification approaches to aggression prevention and control. In Center for Research on Aggression (Eds.), *Prevention and control of aggression*. New York: Pergamon Press.

Goldstein, A. P., Glick, B., Zimmerman, D., Reiner, S., Coultry, T. A., & Gold, D. (1985). *Aggression replacement training: A comprehensive intervention for the acting out delinquent*. Unpublished manuscript.

Goldstein, A. P., & Pentz, M. A. (1984). Psychological skill training and the aggressive adolescent. *School Psychology Review, 13*(3), 311–323.

Goldstein, A. P., Sherman, M. N., Gershaw, N. J., Sprafkin, R. P., & Glick, B. (1978). Training aggressive adolescents in prosocial behavior. *Journal of Youth and Adolescence, 7*(1), 73–92.

Goldstein, A. P., Sprafkin, R. R., Gershaw, N. J., & Klein, P. (1980). *Skillstreaming the adolescent: A structured learning approach to teaching prosocial skills*. Champaign, IL: Research Press.

Goodwin, S., & Mahoney, M. J. (1975). Modification of aggression via modeling: An experimental probe. *Journal of Behavior Therapy and Experimental Psychiatry, 6*, 200–202.

Gottman, J. M. & Leiblum, S. R. (1974). *How to do psychotherapy and how to evaluate it: A manual for beginners*. New York: Holt, Rinehart & Winston Inc.

Gross, A. M., Brigham, T., Hopper, C., & Bologna, W. (1980). Self-management and social skills training: A study with pre-delinquent and delinquent youths. *Criminal Justice and Behavior, 7*(2), 161–183.

Hamberger, K., & Lohr, J. M. (1980). Rational restructuring for anger control: A quasi-experimental case study. *Cognitive Therapy and Research, 4*, 99–102.

Henshaw, S. P., Henker, B., & Whalen, C. K. (1984). Self-control in hyperactive boys in anger inducing situations: Effects of cognitive-behavioral training and of methylphenidate. *Journal of Abnormal Child Psychology, 12*(1), 55–77.

Heppner, P. P. (1978). A review of the problem solving literature and its relationship to the counseling process. *Journal of Clinical Psychology, 25*, 366–375.

Heppner, P. P. (1982). Utilizing a personal problem solving inventory. *Journal of Counseling Psychology, 29*, 66–75.

Hersen, M., & Barlow, H. D. (1976). *Single-case experimental designs: Strategies for studying*. New York: Pergamon Press.

Hobbs, T. R., & Holt, M. M. (1976). The effects of token reinforcement on the behavior of delinquents in cottage settings. *Journal of Applied Behavior Analysis, 9*, 189–198.

Hoshmand, L. T., & Austin, G. W. (1985). *Validation studies of a multi-factor cognitive-behavioral anger control inventory*. Unpublished manuscript.

Jesness, C. (1966). *Jesness inventory* (manual). Palo Alto, CA: Consulting Psychologists Press.

Johnston, L. D., Bachman, J. G., & O'Malley, P. M. (1981). *Student drug use in America 1975–1981*. Washington, DC: U.S. Government Printing Office.

Kagan, J. (1966). Reflection-impulsivity: The generality and dynamics of conceptual tempo. *Journal of Abnormal Psychology, 71*, 17–24.

Kalfus, G. (1984). Peer mediated intervention: A critical review. *Child and Family Behavior Therapy, 6*(1), 17–43.

Karoly, P. (1981). Self-management problems in children. In E. J. Mash & L. G. Terdal (Eds.), *Behavioral assessment of childhood disorders*. New York: Guilford Press.

Kaufman, K. F., & O'Leary, K. D. (1972). Reward, cost, and self-evaluation procedures for disruptive adolescents in a psychiatric hospital school. *Journal of Applied Behavior Analysis, 5*, 293–309.

Kaufmann, L. M., & Wagner, B. R. (1972). Barb: A systematic treatment technology for temper control disorders. *Behavior Therapy, 3*, 84–90.

Kazdin, A. E., Eisenveldt-Dawson, K., & Matson, J. C. (1982). Changes in children's social skills performance as a function of preassessment experience. *Journal of Clinical Child Psychology, 11,* 243–248.

Kendall, P. C. (1981). One year follow-up of concrete versus conceptual cognitive-behavioral, self-control training. *Journal of Consulting and Clinical Psychology, 49,* 748–749.

Kendall, P. C., & Braswell, L. (1985). *Cognitive-behavioral therapy for impulsive children.* New York: Guilford Press.

Kendall, P. C., & Braswell, L. (1982). Cognitive-behavioral self-control therapy for children: A components analysis. *Journal of Consulting and Clinical Psychology, 50,* 672–689.

Kendall, P. C., & Wilcox, L. (1979). Self-control in children: Development of a rating scale. *Journal of Consulting and Clinical Psychology, 47,* 1020–1029.

Kendall, P. C., & Williams, C. L. (1982). Assessing the cognitive and behavioral components of children's self-management. In P. Karoly & F. Kanfer (Eds.), *Self-management and behavior change: From theory to practice.* New York: Pergamon Press.

Kennedy, R. E. (1982). Cognitive-behavioral approaches to the modification of aggressive behavior in children. *School Psychology Review, 11*(1), 47–55.

Kennedy, R. E. (1984). Cognitive behavioral interventions with delinquents. In A. W. Meyers & W. E. Craighead (Eds.), *Cognitive behavior therapy with children.* New York: Plenum.

Kettlewell, P. W., & Dausch, D. F. (1983). The generalization of the effects of a cognitive-behavioral treatment program for aggressive children. *Journal of Abnormal Child Psychology, 11* (1), 101–114.

Kifer, R. E., Lewis, N. A., Green, D. R., & Phillips, E. L. (1974). Training predelinquent youths and their parents to negotiate conflict situations. *Journal of Applied Behavior Analysis, 7,* 357–364.

Kohn, M., Koretsky, M. B., & Haft, M. S. (1979). An adolescent symptom checklist for juvenile delinquents. *Journal of Abnormal Child Psychology, 7*(1), 15–29.

Kolko, D. J., Dorsett, P. G., & Milan, M. A. (1981). A total assessment approach to the evaluation of social skills training: The effectiveness of an anger control program for adolescent psychiatric patients. *Behavioral Assessment, 3,* 383–402.

Lane, T. W., & Burchard, J. D. (1983). Failure to modify delinquent behavior: A constructive analysis. In E. B. Foa & P. M. G. Emmelkamp (Eds.), *Failures in Behavior Therapy.* New York: John Wiley & Sons.

Lange, A., & Jakubowski, P. (1976). *Responsible assertive behavior.* Champaign, IL: Research Press.

Lee, D. Y., Hallberg, E. T., & Hassard, J. H. (1979). Effects of assertion training on aggressive behavior of adolescents. *Journal of Consulting Psychology, 26*(5), 459–461.

Lipinski, D., & Nelson, R. (1974). The reactivity and unreliability of self-recording. *Journal of Consulting and Clinical Psychology, 42,* 118–123.

Little, V. L., & Kendall, P. C. (1979). Cognitive-behavioral interventions with delinquents: Problem-solving, role-taking and self-control. In P. C. Kendall & S. D. Hollon (Eds.), *Cognitive-behavioral interventions: Theory, research and practice.* New York: Academic Press.

Lochman, J. E. (1984). Psychological characteristics and assessment of aggressive adolescents. In C. R. Keith (Ed.), *The aggressive adolescent: Clinical perspectives.* New York: The Free Press.

Lochman, J. E., Burch, P. R., Curry, J. F., & Lampron, L. B. (1984). Treatment and generalization effects of cognitive-behavioral and goal setting interventions with aggressive boys. *Journal of Consulting and Clinical Psychology, 52*(5), 915–916.

Lochman, J. E., Nelson, W. M., III, & Sims, J. P. (1981, Fall). A cognitive-behavioral program for use with aggressive children. *Journal of Clinical Child Psychology,* 146–148.

Long, S. J., & Sherer, M. (1984). Social skills training with juvenile offenders. *Child and Family Behavior Therapy, 6*(4), 1–11.

Lyman, R. D., Rickard, H. C., & Elder, I. R. (1975). Contingency management of self-report and cleaning behavior. *Journal of Abnormal Child Psychology, 3,* 155–162.

Mason, J. (1980). *Guide to stress reduction.* CA: Peace Press.

McCullough, J., Huntsinger, G., & Nay, W. (1977). Self-control treatment of aggression in a 16-year-old male: Case study. *Journal of Consulting and Clinical Psychology, 45,* 322–331.

Meichenbaum, D. (1975). A self-instructional approach to stress management: A proposal for stress inoculation training. In C. Spielberger & I. Sarason (Eds.), *Stress & Anxiety* (Vol. 2). New York: John Wiley & Sons.

Meichenbaum, D., & Cameron, R. (1972). *Stress inoculation: A skills training approach to anxiety management.* Unpublished manuscript, University of Waterloo, Waterloo, Ontario.

Meichenbaum, D. H., & Goodman, J. (1971). Training impulsive children to talk to themselves. *Journal of Abnormal Psychology, 77*(2), 115–126.

Meichenbaum, D., & Jaremko, M. (1983). *Stress reduction and prevention.* New York: Plenum.

Merritt, R. E., & Walley, D. D. (1977). *The group leader's handbook: Resources, techniques, and survival skills.* Champaign, IL: Research Press.

Moon, J. R., & Eisler, R. M. (1983). Anger control: An experimental comparison of three behavioral treatments. *Behavior Therapy, 14*(4), 493–505.

Moss, G. R., & Rick, G. R. (1981). Application of a token economy for adolescents in a private psychiatric hospital. *Behavior Therapy, 12,* 585–590.

Nasby, W., Hayden, B., & DePaulo, B. M. (1980). Attributional bias among aggressive boys to interpret unambiguous social stimuli as displays of hostility. *Journal of Abnormal Psychology, 89,* 459–468.

Neilans, T. H., & Israel, A. C. (1981). Towards maintenance and generalization of behavior change: Teaching children self-regulation and self-instruction skills. *Cognitive Therapy and Research, 5,* 189–196.

Nomellini, S., & Katz, R. (1983). Effects of anger control training on abusive parents. *Cognitive Therapy and Research, 7,* 57–68.

Novaco, R. W. (1975). *Anger control: The development and evaluation of an experimental treatment.* Lexington, MA: D.C. Heath & Co.

Novaco, R. W. (1977a). Stress inoculation: A cognitive therapy for anger and its application to a case of depression. *Journal of Consulting and Clinical Psychology, 45*(4), 600–608.

Novaco, R. W. (1977b). A stress inoculation approach to anger management in the training of law enforcement officers. *American Journal of Community Psychology, 5,* 327–346.

Novaco, R. W. (1979). The cognitive regulation of anger and stress. In P. Kendall & S. Hollon (Eds.), *Cognitive-behavioral interventions: Theory, research and procedures.* New York: Academic Press.

Novaco, R. W. (1980). Training of probation counselors for anger problems. *Journal of Counseling Psychology, 27,* 385–390.

Novaco, R. W. (1985). Anger and its therapeutic regulation. In M. A. Chesney & R. H. Rosenman (Eds.), *Anger and hostility in cardiovascular and behavioral disorders.* New York: Hemisphere Publishing Corp.

Oas, P. (1983). Impulsive behavior and assessment of impulsivity with hospitalized adolescents. *Psychological Reports, 53,* 764–766.

O'Leary, S., & Dubey, D. R. (1979). Applications of self-control procedures by children: A review. *Journal of Applied Behavior Analysis, 121,* 449–465.

Ollendick, T. H., & Cerny, J. A. (1981). *Clinical behavior therapy with children.* New York: Plenum.

Ollendick, T., & Hersen, M. (1979). Social skills training for juvenile delinquents. *Behavior Research and Therapy, 17,* 547–554.

Olweus, D. (1979). Stability of aggressive reaction patterns in males: A review. *Psychological Bulletin, 86,* 852–875.

Olweus, D. (1980) Familial and temperamental determinants of aggressive behavior in adolescent boys: A causal analysis. *Developmental Psychology, 16*(6), 644–660.

Ostrov, E., Marohn, R. C., Offer, D., Curtiss, G., & Feczko, M. (1980). The adolescent antisocial behavior checklist. *Journal of Clinical Psychology, 36*(2), 594–601.

Patterson, G. R. (1975). *Families: Applications of social learning to family.* Champaign, IL: Research Press.

Patterson, G. R., Reid, J. G., Jones, R. R., & Conger, R. E. (1975). *A social learning approach to family intervention* (Vol. 1). Eugene, OR: Catalise Publishing.

Pentz, M. A., & Kazdin, A. E. (1982). Assertion modeling and stimuli effects on assertive behavior and self-efficacy in adolescents. *Behavior Research and Therapy, 20*(4), 365–374.

Peterson, L. (1983). Failures in self-control. In E. B. Foa & P. M. G. Emmelkamp (Eds.), *Failures in behavior therapy.* New York: John Wiley & Sons.

Phillips, E. L., Phillips, E. A., Fixsen, D. L., & Wolf, M. M. (1974). *The Teaching Family Handbook.* Lawrence, KS: University Printing Service.

Phillips, J. S., & Ray, R. S. (1980). Behavioral approaches to childhood disorders. *Behavior Modification, 4*, 3–34.

Platt, J. J., Spivack, G., Altman, N., Altman, D., & Peizer, S. V. (1974). Adolescent problem solving thinking. *Journal of Clinical Child Psychology, 42*, 787–793.

Porteus, S. D. (1955). *The maze test: Recent advances.* Palo Alto, CA: Pacific Books.

Prinz, R. J., Foster, S., Kent, R. N., & O'Leary, K. D. (1979). Multivariate assessment of conflict in distressed and nondistressed mother–adolescent dyads. *Journal of Applied Behavior Analysis, 12*, 691–700.

Prinz, R. J., Swan, G., Leibert, D., Weintraub, S., & Neale, J. M. (1978). ASSESS: Adjustment scales for sociometric evaluation of secondary-school students. *Journal of Abnormal Child Psychology, 6*, 493–501.

Quay, H. C. (1977). Measuring dimensions of deviant behavior: The behavior problem checklist. *Journal of Abnormal Child Psychology, 5*, 277–287.

Quick, J., Francis, M., Hernandez, M., & Freedman, R. (1980, November). *Teaching appropriate anger expression to the multi-problem adolescent in a day treatment setting.* Paper presented at the Annual Meeting of the Association for Advancement of Behavior Therapy, New York.

Rachal, J. V., Maisto, S. A., Guess, L. L., & Hubbard, R. L. (1982). Alcohol use among youth. *Alcohol and Health* (Monograph No. 1). Washington, DC: U.S. Government Printing Office.

Rahaim, S., LeFebvre, C., & Jenkins, J. O. (1980). The effects of social skills training on behavioral and cognitive components of anger management. *Journal of Behavior Therapy and Experimental Psychiatry, 11*, 3–8.

Randall, R. W. (1985). *Behavior management techniques: Interpersonal intervention.* Utica, NY: R.W. Randall and Associates.

Richards, C. S. (1978). When self-control fails: A case study of the maintenance problem in self-control treatment programs. *Cognitive Therapy and Research, 2*, 397–401.

Robin, A. L. (1981). A controlled evaluation of problem-solving communication training with parent-adolescent conflict. *Behavior Therapy, 12*, 593–609.

Robin, A. L., Fischel, J. E., & Brown, K. E. (1985). The measurement of self-control in children: Validation of the self-control rating scale. *Journal of Pediatric Psychology, 9*, 165–175.

Robin, A. L., & Foster, S. L. (1984). Problem solving communication training: A behavioral-family systems approach to parent-adolescent conflict. In P. Karoly & J. J. Steffen (Eds.), *Adolescent behavior disorders: Foundations and contemporary concerns.* Lexington, MA: Lexington Books/ D.C. Heath & Co.

Robin, A. L., Kent, R., O'Leary, K. D., Foster, S., & Prinz, R. (1977). An approach to teaching parents and adolescents problem solving communication skills: A preliminary report. *Behavior Therapy, 8*, 639–643.

Robin, A. L., Schneider, M., & Dolnick, M. (1976). The turtle technique: An extended case study of self-control in the classroom. *Psychology in the Schools, 12*, 120–128.

Rosenbaum, M. (1980). A schedule for assessing self-control behaviors: Preliminary findings. *Behavior Therapy, 11*, 109–121.

Rosenbaum, N. S., & Drabman, R. S. (1984). " . . . But I'd rather do it myself:" A review of self-control techniques in the classroom. *Journal of Applied Behavior Analysis, 17*, 467–485.

Rule, B. G., & Nesdale, A. R. (1976). Emotional arousal and aggressive behavior. *Psychological Bulletin, 83*, 851–861.

Sanchez-Craig, B. M. (1976). Cognitive and behavioral coping strategies in the reappraisal of stressful social situations. *Journal of Counseling Psychology, 23*(1), 7–12.

Sanders, M. A. (1978). Behavioral self-control training with children and adolescents: A review and critical analysis of educational applications. *The Exceptional Child, 25*(2), 83–103.

Santogrossi, D. A., O'Leary, K. D., Romanczy!, R. G., & Kaufman, K. F. (1973). Self-evaluation by adolescents in a psychiatric hospital school token programs. *Journal of Applied Behavior Analysis, 6,* 277–287.

Santostefano, S., & Rieder, C. (1984). Cognitive controls and aggression in children. *Journal of Consulting and Clinical Psychology, 52,* 46–56.

Sarason, I. G., & Sarason, B. R. (1981). Teaching cognitive and social skills to high school students. *Journal of Consulting and Clinical Psychology, 49*(6), 908–918.

Saylor, C. F., Benson, B., & Einhaus, L. (1985). Evaluation of an anger management program for aggressive boys in inpatient treatment. *Journal of Child and Adolescent Psychotherapy, 2,* 5–15.

Schinke, S. P. (1981). Interpersonal skills training with adolescents. In M. Hersen, R. M. Eisler, & P. M. Miller (Eds.), *Progress in behavior modification, Volume II.* New York: Academic Press.

Schlesser, R., Meyers, A., & Cohen, R. (1981). Generalization of self-instructions. Effects of general versus specific content, active rehearsal and cognitive level. *Child Development, 52,* 335–340.

Schlichter, K. J., & Horan, J. J. (1981). Effects of stress inoculation on the anger and aggression management of institutionalized juvenile delinquents. *Cognitive Therapy and Research, 5*(4), 359–365.

Schrader, C., Long, J., Panzer, C., Gillet, D., & Kornblath, R. (1977, December). *An anger control package for adolescent drug abusers.* Paper presented at the 11th Annual Convention of the Association for Advancement of Behavior Therapy, Atlanta.

Schultz, J., & Lutne, W. (1959). *Autogenic training.* New York: Grune & Stratton.

Seymour, F. W., & Stokes, T. F. (1976). Self-recording in training girls to increase work and evoke staff praise in an institution for offenders. *Journal of Applied Behavior Analysis, 9,* 41–54.

Shelton, J. L., & Levy, R. L. (1981). *Behavioral assignments and treatment compliance.* Champaign, IL: Research Press.

Shure, M. B., & Spivack, G. (1972). Means-ends thinking, adjustment, and social class among elementary school-aged children. *Journal of Consulting and Clinical Psychology, 38,* 348–353.

Simon, S., Howe, L., & Kuschenbaum, H. (1972). *Values clarification.* New York: Holt, Rinehart & Winston.

Snyder, J., & White, M. (1979). The use of cognitive self-instruction in the treatment of behaviorally disturbed adolescents. *Behavior Therapy, 10,* 227–235.

Spence, S. H., & Marzillier, J. S. (1981). Social skills training with adolescent male offenders—II: Short-term, long-term and generalized effects. *Behaviour Research and Therapy, 19,* 349–368.

Spirito, A., Finch, A. J., Smith, T., & Cooley, W. (1981). Stress inoculation for anger and anxiety control: A case study with an emotionally disturbed boy. *Journal of Child Clinical Psychology, 10,* 67–70.

Spivack, G., Platt, J., & Shure, M. (1976). *The problem solving approach to adjustment.* San Francisco: Jossey-Bass.

Stermac, L. (1984). *Cognitive behavioral treatment for anger control in a forensic population.* Paper presented at the Association for Advancement of Behavior Therapy, Philadelphia.

Stokes, T. F., & Baer, D. M. (1977). An implicit technology of generalization. *Journal of Applied Behavior Analysis, 10,* 349–368.

Stumphauzer, J. (1976). Elimination of stealing by self-reinforcement of alternative behavior and family contracting. *Journal of Behavior Therapy and Experimental Psychiatry, 7,* 265–268.

Stumphauzer, J. (1979). *Progress in behavior therapy with delinquents.* Springfield, IL: Charles C Thomas.

Stumphauzer, J. (1981). Behavioral approaches to juvenile delinquency: Future perspectives. In L. Michelson, M. Hersen, & S. M. Turner (Eds.), *Future perspectives in behavior therapy*. New York: Plenum.

Thackwray, O., Meyers, A., Schlesser, R., & Cohen, R. (1985). Achieving generalization with general versus specific self-instructions. Effects on academically deficient children. *Cognitive Therapy and Research, 9,* 297–308.

Thelen, M. H., Fry, R. A., Dollinger, S., & Paul, S. (1976). Use of videotaped models to improve the interpersonal adjustments of delinquents. *Journal of Consulting and Clinical Psychology, 44,* 492.

Thelen, M. H., Fry R. A., Fehrenbach, P. A., & Frautschi, N. M. (1979). Therapeutic videotape and film modeling: A review. *Psychological Bulletin, 86*(4), 701–720.

Vaal, J. J. (1975). The Rathus Assertiveness Schedule: Reliability at the junior high level. *Behavior Therapy, 6,* 566–567.

Varley, W. H. (1984). Behavior modification approaches to the aggressive adolescent. In C. R. Keith (Ed.), *The aggressive adolescent: Clinical perspectives*. New York: The Free Press.

Warren, D., & Mchellan, A. (1982). Systematic desensitization as a treatment for maladaptive anger and aggression: A review. *Psychological Reports,* 1095–1103.

Weathers, L., & Liberman, R. (1975). Contingency contracting with families of delinquent adolescents. *Behavior Therapy, 6,* 356–366.

Williams, D. J., & Akamatsu, T. J. (1978). Cognitive self-guidance with juvenile delinquents. *Cognitive Therapy and Research, 2,* 285–288.

Wilson, R. (1984). A review of self-control treatment for aggressive behavior. *Behavioral Disorders, 9,* 131–140.

Wodarski, J. (1979). Follow-up on behavioral intervention with troublesome adolescents. *Journal of Behavior Therapy and Experimental Psychiatry, 10,* 181–188.

Wolfe, D. A., Kaufman, K., Aragona, J., & Sandler, J. (1981). *The child management program for abusive parents*. Winter Park, FL: Anna Publishing.

Wolfe, D. A., Sandler, J., & Kaufman, K. (1981). A competency-based parent training program for child abusers. *Journal of Consulting and Clinical Psychology, 49,* 633–640.

Wolpe, J. (1973). *The practice of behavior therapy* (2nd ed.). Oxford: Pergamon Press.

Wood, R., & Flynn, J. M. (1978). A self-evaluation token system versus an external evaluation token system alone in a residential setting with predelinquent youth. *Journal of Applied Behavior Analysis, 11*(4), 503–512.

Author Index

Subject Index

About the Authors

Eva L. Feindler earned her MA and PhD at West Virginia University in Clinical Child Psychology. In 1979, following her clinical internship at the Children's Psychiatric Center in Eatontown, New Jersey, she began teaching at Adelphi University, Garden City, New York. Currently an Associate Professor of Psychology, she directs the MA Program in Applied Psychology: Behavioral Technology Specialty. Actively engaged in training and supervision of graduate students, Dr. Feindler conducts numerous community workshops and training programs in behavior therapy and behavior modification for stress-related disorders. She has served as a consultant for the New York City Board of Special Education and Sagamore Children's Center. She also served as the Fundamentals Course Coordinator for the Association for Advancement of Behavior Therapy. Further, she is an Associate Director of the Institute for Behavior Therapy in Greenvale, Long Island. Dr. Feindler has conducted numerous applied research evaluations in the area of stress and anger control and has co-authored several published research reports.

Randolph Brooks Ecton is currently completing his master's degree in applied psychology at Adelphi University. He is also a staff psychologist at Sagamore Children's Center, Melville, New York, where he was responsible for the development and implementation of the hospital's group and individual anger control programs. He received the Executive Director's Award for "the innovative and outstanding contribution given to the children of Sagamore through the development of the Anger Control Program." He was Sagamore's OMH Outstanding Employee nominee for 1983. The Anger Control Program he developed at Sagamore is currently being considered for the Annual OMH Recognition Award for Children and Youth. Mr. Ecton has previously served as a psychology consultant for the Great Neck/Manhasset Head Start Program; research assistant for the Family Crisis Program at North Shore University Hospital; recreation therapist at the Cerebral Palsy Center in Roosevelt, New York; and caseworker and project supervisor for Barrett Learning Center for Boys in Hanover, Virginia.

Psychology Practitioner Guidebooks

Editors
Arnold P. Goldstein, Syracuse University
Leonard Krasner, SUNY at Stony Brook
Sol L. Garfield, Washington University